Mind Is a Myth

My teaching, if that is the word you want to use, has no copyright. You are free to reproduce, distribute, interpret, misinterpret, distort, garble, do what you like, even claim authorship, without my consent or the permission of anybody.

Mind Is a Myth

Disquieting Conversations with the
Man Called U.G.

U.G. Krishnamurti

Edited by Terry Newland

SENTIENT PUBLICATIONS

First Sentient Publications Edition 2007

Printed in the United States of America

Cover design by Kim Johansen, Black Dog Design
Book design by Adam Schnitzmeier

Library of Congress Cataloging-in-Publication Data

Krishnamurti, U. G. (Uppaluri Gopala)
  Mind is a myth : disquieting conversations with the man called U.G. /
U.G. Krishnamurti ; edited by Terry Newland.
      p. cm.
  "Consists of edited talks between U.G. Krishnamurti and various
questioners in India, Switzerland and California in 1983 and 1984"--P.
  ISBN 978-1-59181-065-0
  1. Krishnamurti, U. G. (Uppaluri Gopala)--Interviews. 2.
Philosophers--India--Interviews. 3.   Philosophy of mind. 4.   Spiritual
life.
  I. Newland, Terry. II. Title.

B5134.K765A3 2007
181'.4--dc22

                          2007013428

10 9 8 7 6 5 4 3 2 1

SENTIENT PUBLICATIONS
A Limited Liablility Company
1113 Spruce St.
Boulder, CO 80302
www.sentientpublications.com

Other books by U.G. Krishnamurti

The Courage to Stand Alone

The Mystique of Enlightenment

Thought Is Your Enemy

No Way Out

The Natural State

The Little Book of Questions

This book consists of edited talks between U.G. Krishnamurti and various questioners in India, Switzerland, and California in 1983 and 1984.

Contents

Introduction

Here at the eleventh hour is a refreshing, radical, and unconventional appraisal of the entire human enterprise. In his previous work, The Mystique of Enlightenment, U.G. Krishnamurti took close aim right between the eyes of the status quo, and fired away. In this new book he makes even shorter work of traditional values and thinking, lobbing grenades, as it were, into the very citadels of our most cherished beliefs and aspirations. For the seekers of God, Happiness, or Enlightenment this book has very little to recommend it. But for those who grow weary of the search and have developed a well-tempered skepticism, this little volume may prove invaluable. This is the story of a man who had it all—looks, wealth, culture, fame, travel, career—and gave it all up to find for himself the answer to his burning question, "Is there actually anything like freedom, enlightenment, or liberation behind all the abstractions the religions have thrown at us?" He never got an answer.

There are no answers to questions like that. U.G. casts philosophy into an entirely new mold. For him philosophy is neither the love of wisdom nor the avoidance of error, but the disappearance of all philosophical questions. Says U.G.:

When the questions you have resolve themselves into just one question, your question, then that question must detonate, explode, and disappear entirely, leaving behind a smoothly functioning biological organism, free of the distortion and interference of the separative thinking structure.

U.G.'s message is a shocking one: we are all on the wrong train, on the wrong track, going in the wrong direction. When the time comes to face up to the catastrophe of man's present crisis, you will find U.G. at the head of the line, ready and able to demolish the carefully built assumptions so dear and consoling to us all. A U.G. sampler: making love is war; cause-and-effect is the shibboleth of confused minds; *yoga* and health foods destroy the body; the body and not the soul is immortal; there is no communism in Russia, no freedom in America, and no spirituality in India; service to mankind is utter selfishness; Jesus was another misguided Jew, and the Buddha was a crackpot; mutual terror, not love, will save mankind; attending church and going to the bar for a drink are identical; there is nothing inside you but fear; communication is impossible between human beings; God, Love, Happiness, the unconscious, death, reincarnation, and the soul are non-existent figments of our rich imagination; Freud is the fraud of the 20th century, while J. Krishnamurti is its greatest phony.

The man's fearless willingness to brush aside all the accumulated knowledge and wisdom of the past is nothing short of stupendous. In this regard he is a colossus, a walking and talking "Siva," ready to destroy all so that life can move on with new vigor and freedom. His ruthless, unremitting attack on our most cherished ideas and institutions amounts to no less than an insurrection in consciousness; a corrupt superstructure, tainted at the core, is unceremoniously blown apart and nothing is put in its place. Taking great delight in the act of sheer annihilation, U.G. offers his listeners *nothing*, but rather, takes away all they have so laboriously and unwittingly accumulated. If the old must be destroyed before the new can be, then U.G. is, indeed, the harbinger of a new beginning for man.

Society, which, as Aldous Huxley pointed out, is organized lovelessness, can make no place for a free man like U.G. Krishnamurti. He does not fit into any known social structure, spiritual or secular. Society, which uses its members as a means to ensure its own continuity, cannot help but be threatened by a man like U.G., a devout disestablishmentarian who has nothing to protect, no following to satisfy, no interest in respectability, and who habitually speaks the most disillusioning truths no matter what the consequences.

U.G. is a "finished" man. In him there is no search, and therefore no destiny. His life now consists of a series of disjointed events. There is no center to his life, no one "conducting" his life, no inner shadow, no "ghost in the machine." What is there is a calm, smoothly functioning, highly intelligent and responsive biological machine, nothing more. One looks in vain for evidence of a self, psyche, or ego; there is only the simple functioning of a sensitive organism. It is little wonder that such a "finished" man would discard the banal, tarnished commonalities of science, religion, politics, and philosophy and instead bear directly into the heart of matters, presenting his case simply, fearlessly, forcefully, and without corroboration, to any who wish to listen.

The subject of this work, Mr. Uppaluri Gopala Krishnamurti[1] was born of middle-class Brahmin parents on the morning of July 9, 1918, in the village of Masulipatam, South India. As far as we know there were no peculiar events surrounding his birth, celestial or otherwise. His mother died of puerperal fever seven days after giving birth to her first and only child. Upon her death bed she implored the maternal grandfather of the boy to take special care of him, adding that she was certain that he had a great and important destiny before him.

The grandfather took this prediction, and his daughter's request, very seriously, and vowed to give the boy all the advantages of a wealthy Brahmin "prince." The father soon remarried, leaving U.G. to be cared for by the grandparents. The grandfather was an ardent Theosophist and knew J. Krishnamurti, Annie Besant, Col. Alcott, and the other leaders of the Theosophical Society. U.G. was to meet all these people in his youth and was to spend most of his formative years around Adyar, the world headquarters of the Theosophical Society, in Madras, India. U.G. says of that time: "My grandfather kept a sort of open house into which were invited traveling monks and renunciates, religious scholars, *pundits*, various *gurus, mahatmas,* and *swamis.*" There were endless discussions on philosophy, comparative religions, occultism, and metaphysics. Every wall of the house was covered with famous Hindu and Theosophical leaders, especially J. Krishnamurti. The boy's childhood was, in short, steeped in religious lore, philosophical discourse, and the influence of various spiritual personages. All this appealed to the boy greatly. He even begged one traveling guru, who arrived with a huge retinue of camels, disciples and attendants, to take him away with him so that he might become a student of his spiritual teaching. The boy U.G. was taken by the grandfather all over India to visit holy places and people, *ashramas*, retreats, and centers of learning. He spent seven summers in the Himalayas studying classical yoga with a famous adept, Swami Sivananda.

It was in these early years of his life that U.G. began to feel that "something was wrong somewhere," referring to the whole religious tradition into which he had been immersed almost from the beginning. His yoga master, a strict and self-righteous figure of authority, was startled when U.G. found him behind closed doors devouring some hot pickles forbidden for yogis. U.G., just a boy, said to himself, "How can this man deceive himself and others, pretending to be one thing while doing another?" He gave up his yoga practices, maintaining a healthy skepticism towards all things spiritual on into his adulthood.

More and more he wanted to "do things *my* way," questioning the authority of others over him. Breaking from the traditions of his Brahminic background, he tore from his body the sacred thread, symbol of his religious heritage. He became a young cynic, rejecting the spiritual conventions of his culture and questioning everything for himself. He displayed less and less respect for the religious institutions and customs thought so important by his family and community. In him developed a healthy disdain for his religious inheritance, a disdain which was to develop into an acute sense of what he was later to call "the hypocrisy of the holy business." His grandmother said of him that he "had the heart of a butcher." All this allowed him time to develop the tremendous courage and insight necessary to brush aside the entire psychological and genetic content of his past.

By the age of twenty-one U.G. had become a quasi-atheist, studying secular western philosophy and psychology at the University of Madras. At this juncture he was asked by a friend to go with him to visit the famous "Sage of Arunachala," Bhagavan Sri Ramana Maharshi, at his ashram at Tiruvannamalai, not far south of Madras. In the year 1939 U.G. reluctantly went. He was convinced by that time that all holy men were phonies and were taking people for a ride. But to his surprise Ramana Maharshi was different. The Bhagavan, a serene, doe-eyed sage of the highest wisdom and integrity, could not but make a strong impression on the young U.G. He rarely spoke to those who approached him with questions. U.G. approached the Bhagavan with some trepidation and misgivings, putting to the master three questions:

"Is there," asked U.G., "anything like enlightenment?"

"Yes, there is," replied the master.

"Are there any levels to it?"

The Bhagavan replied, "No, no levels are possible. It is all one thing. Either you are there or you are not there at all."

Finally U.G. asked, "This thing called enlightenment, can you give it to me?"

Looking the serious young man in the eyes he replied, "Yes, I can give it, *but can you take it?*"

From that time on U.G. was haunted by this reply and relenlessly queried himself, *"What* is it that I can't take?" He resolved then and there that whatever the Maharshi was talking about, he "could take it." He was later to say that this encounter was to change the course of his life and "put me back on the track." He never visited the Bhagavan again. Ramana Maharshi died, incidentally, in 1951, of cancer, and is regarded as one of the greatest sages India has ever produced.

By his mid-twenties sex had become a problem for U.G. Although intermittently vowing to forego sex and marriage in deference to the life of a religious celibate, he eventually reasoned that sex was a natural drive, that it was not wise to suppress it, and that, anyhow, society had provided legitimate institutions to fulfill this urge. He chose as his bride one of three young beautiful Brahmin women his grandmother had selected for him as possible suitable mates. He was to say later, "I awoke the morning after my wedding night and knew without doubt that I had made the biggest mistake of my life." He remained married for seventeen years, fathering four children. From the very beginning he wanted out of the marriage, but somehow children kept coming and the married life continued. His oldest son, Vasant, came down with polio, and U.G. decided to move the family to the United States so that the boy could receive the best treatment. In the process he spent nearly all his fortune that he had received from his grandfather. His hope was that he could get some higher education for his wife, find her a job, and put her in an independent position so that he could go on alone. This he did, finding her a job with the World Book Encyclopedia. By this time his fortune had run out, and he was fed up with being a public speaker (first on behalf of the Theosophical Society and later as an independent platform orator), his marriage was finished, and he was losing interest in the struggle to be somebody in this world. By his early forties he was broke, alone, and all but forgotten by his friends and associates. He began wandering, first in New York City, then in London, where he was reduced to spending his days in the London Library to escape the English winter cold, and giving Indian cooking lessons for a little money. Then on to Paris, where his wanderings continued. Of that period in his life U.G. was later to say:

> I was like a leaf blown about by a fickle wind, with neither past nor future, neither family nor career, nor any sort of spiritual fulfillment. I was slowly losing my will power to do anything. I was not rejecting or renouncing the world; it was just drifting away from me and I was unable and unwilling to hold onto it.

Broke and alone, he wandered to Geneva where he had left a few francs in an old account, enough possibly to get him by for a few days. Then that little money ran out, his rent became due, and he was left with nowhere to turn. He decided to go to the Indian Consulate there in Geneva and ask to be repatriated to India. "I had no money, no friends, and no will left. I thought that at least they can't turn me out of India. I am, after all, a citizen. Perhaps I can just sit under a banyan tree somewhere and maybe someone will feed me." So, at the age of forty-five, a complete failure in the eyes of the world, penniless and alone, he walked into the Consulate and begged to be returned to his homeland. He had little choice. This was to be a turning point in his life.

U.G. walked into the Indian Consulate office in Geneva and began telling his sad story to the consul there. The more he talked, the more fascinated the consul became. Soon the whole office was in a hushed silence listening to his remarkable tale. A secretary-translator in the office, Valentine de Kerven[2], was listening intently. Already in her early sixties, she had much experience of the world, and took pity on the strange charismatic man. No one in the office knew what to do with him, so Valentine volunteered to put him up in her place for a few days until the consul could figure out something.

Valentine, no stranger to adversity herself, sympathized with the wandering, destitute man, and soon offered him a home in Europe. She had a small inheritance and pension which was sufficient for them both. U.G., loath to return to India and face his family, friends, and poor prospects, gratefully accepted the offer. The next four years (1963-67) were halcyon days for them. She left her job at the consulate and lived quietly with U.G., moving with the weather to Italy, the south of France, Paris, and Switzerland. Later they began spending their winters in south India where things were relatively inexpensive and the weather more benign. During these years U.G., as he later explained, did nothing. "I slept, read the Time Magazine, ate, and went for walks with Valentine or alone. That was all." He was in a sort of incubation period. His search had nearly come to an end. He never mentioned to Valentine the occult powers, spiritual experiences, and religious background which constituted so much of his life. They just lived simply and quietly as private migrating householders.

They took to spending their summer months in the converted attic of a 400-year-old chalet in the charming Swiss village of Saanen, in the Bernese Oberland. For some reason J. Krishnamurti decided to hold a series of talks and gatherings in a huge tent erected on the outskirts of the same little town. Religious seekers, yogis, philosophers, and intellectuals from both the east and the west began showing up in the small town to attend the Krishnamurti talks, to give and take yoga instructions, and confer on matters spiritual and philosophical. U.G. and Valentine kept a respectful distance, not wishing to become part of the growing scene which began to resemble more and more a circus.

In this environment U.G. approached his forty-ninth birthday. The Kowmara Nadi, a famous and respected astrological "record" in Madras, had long ago predicted that U.G. would undergo a profound transformation on his forty-ninth birthday. As the day approached, strange, unaccountable things began occurring to U.G. Something radical and utterly unexpected was about to happen to him.

In his thirty-fifth year U.G. had begun to get recurring painful headaches, and, not knowing what to do, began taking large amounts of coffee and aspirin to cope with the excruciating pain.

At this time also he began to look younger instead of older. By the time he was forty-nine he looked to be a man of seventeen or eighteen years. After the age of forty-nine he began ageing once again, although he continues to appear much younger than he is. Between headaches he would go through extraordinary experiences where, as he later described it, "I felt headless, like my head was missing." Arising simultaneously with these strange phenomena were the so-called occult powers, or what U.G. refers to as man's natural powers and instincts. A person could walk into the room and U.G., having never met that person, could see his entire past and history as though reading a living autobiography. He could glance at a stranger's palm and instantly know their destiny. All the occult powers began to manifest themselves in him gradually after the age of thirty-five. "I never used these powers for anything; they were just there. I knew they were of no great importance and just let them be."

Things kept building within him, and U.G., concerned she might conclude that he was mad, never mentioned a thing about these extraordinary developments to Valentine, or anyone for that matter. As his forty-ninth birthday approached he began to have what he later referred to as "panoramic vision," a way of seeing in which the field of vision wrapped around the open eyes in a nearly 360-degree spread, while the viewer or observer disappeared entirely and objects moved right through the head and body. The entire organism, unknown to U.G. at the time, was evidently preparing itself for some calamity or transformation of immense proportions. U.G. did nothing.

On the morning of July the 9th, 1967, his forty-ninth birthday, U.G. went with a friend to hear J. Krishnamurti[3] give a public talk in a large tent on the outskirts of Saanen, the village in which U.G. and Valentine had been living for some time. U.G. had contracted with a publisher to write his autobiography. While working on the book, U.G. came to the part describing his association with J. Krishnamurti. He did not remember much of what he had felt towards the elderly revered "World Teacher" of the Theosophical Society. He had not had contact with J. Krishnamurti for many years and had no definite opinion about the man. So he decided to go to hear the morning talk by J. Krishnamurti to sort of "refresh my memory," as he put it. Midway through the talk, U.G., listening to J. Krishnamurti's description of a free man, suddenly realized that it was himself who was being described. "What the hell am I doing listening to someone describe how I am functioning?" Freedom in consciousness became at that moment no longer something "over there," or "out there," but simply the way he was already physiologically functioning at that very instant. This stunned U.G. so strongly that he left the tent in a somewhat dazed state of mind and walked alone towards his chalet on the other side of the valley. As he approached his chalet he stopped to rest on a small bench which overlooked the beautiful rivers and mountains of Saanen Valley.

While sitting on the bench alone, looking at the green valley and rugged peaks of the Oberland, it occurred to him:

> I have searched everywhere to find an answer to my question "Is there enlightenment?" but have never questioned the search itself. Because I have assumed that goal, enlightenment, exists, I have had to search, and it is the search itself which has been choking me and keeping me out of my natural state. There is no such thing as spiritual or psychological enlightenment because there is no such thing as spirit or psyche at all. I have been a damn fool all my life, searching for something which does not exist. My search is at an end.

At that moment all the questions disappeared and U.G. ceased to act any longer via the separative thought structure. A bit of energy entered his brain through one of the senses and was *left alone*. A bit of energy left alone to vibrate freely, untranslated, uncensored, and unused by a separative, preemptive thought structure is a dangerous thing. It is the very substance of inner anarchy. Being untouched by thought, which is time, it has nowhere to go and can find no escape from the stillness. A tremendous molecular pressure is built up that can have release only in an explosion. That explosion caused within U.G. the collapse of the entire thought structure, and with it the notion of an independent self and an opposing society. He had reached the end of the corridor of opposites; cause and effect ceased altogether. The calamity reached right down to the level of the cells and chromosomes. It was physiological, not psychological, in nature. It implies that at the end of the known is the "Big Bang."

U.G., sitting bewildered and flabbergasted on the little bench, looked down at his body. But this time he looked without the cultural background that identified him as male, Indian, Brahmin, seeker, world traveler, public speaker, civilized gentleman, virtuous person, etc., seeing instead a warm-blooded mammal, a calm, harmless, fully-clothed "monkey." The slate had been miraculously wiped clean, culture and the self had been utterly undone in a twinkling, and what was left was a graceful, simple, well-mannered "ape"—aware, intelligent, and free of all pretense and self-absorption. Not having the foggiest notion of what was happening to him, he walked the few feet to his chalet and lay down.

Within hours he felt the contractions at various locations on his body—mostly in the brain and at the locations of the nervous plexuses and certain glands—slacken. The body, no longer choked and suppressed by the accumulated knowledge of the past (the separative thought structure), began a full-scale mutation. Large swellings appeared at various sites, including the pituitary, pineal, and thymus glands, the center of the forehead, and the anterior of the throat. The eyes stopped blinking and tear ducts, heretofore dormant, started to function, lubricating eyes in a new way. Various *kundalini* experiences manifested themselves, although U.G. refers to these in purely physiological terms. A sort of combustion or "ionization" of the cells occurred on a daily basis, raising the body temperature to incredible heights and throwing off a sort of ash which could easily be seen on his body. Just as a computer "goes down," U.G. "went down" several times a day, slipping into a death state where the heart-beat would nearly cease, the body's temperature would drop to a level just sufficient to sustain life, and the entire body would get very stiff and moribund. Just before the body reached a complete clinical death state, it would somehow "kick on" again, the pulse would quicken, the temperature would rise to normal, and slow stretching movements, similar to a baby's, would manifest themselves. Within minutes he would be back to functioning normally.

This extraordinary mutation U.G. has come to refer to as his "calamity." It was a tremendous shock to the body to have its suppressor, the separative psychic structure, collapse and entirely disappear. There was no longer a psychic coordinator collating, comparing, and matching all the sensory input so that it could use the body and its relations for its own separative continuity. Events became disjointed and unrelated. The senses, freed from the "pale cast of thought," began their independent careers, and the useful content of thought and culture dropped, as it were, into the background, to be brought forth into consciousness, unencumbered by any sentimental or emotional overtones, only when an objective demand is made upon them, and for the smooth functioning of the material organism. The hands and forearms changed their structure, so that now his hands face backward instead of to the sides. His body is now hermaphroditic, a perfect union of animus-anima, and enjoys a sexuality the likes of which we can only guess. His right side responds to women, his left more to men. The natural flow of energy through his body, no longer blocked and dissipated by contractive thought, flows right up from the spine through the brain, and out the top of the head. His biological sensitivity (and there is no other kind) is so acute that the movements of celestial bodies, especially the moon, have a visibly strong effect on him. "To be affectionate does not mean that you are demonstrative or like to compulsively touch others, but, rather, that you are affected by *everything,*" he says.

These incredible physiological changes continued on for years. He was so bewildered by what had happened to him that he did not speak for a year after the calamity. He had to practically learn to think and talk all over again, so complete was his mutation. After a year or so he had regained most of his communicative powers, yet he did not speak. "What is there to say after a thing like this?" he asked himself. One day the answer came to him in a flash, *"I will say it exactly the way it is."* Except for a year's break in the late '70's, he has been speaking tirelessly ever since. Of all this U.G. now says:

> I did not know what was happening to me. I had no reference point at all. Somehow I died and came back to life free of my past, and thank God for that. This thing happened without my volition and *despite* my religious background, and that is a miracle. It cannot be used as a model and be duplicated by others.

What U.G. is describing in these pages—his natural state—does not represent a new way of living, for living is for us actually a way of getting what we want. If we change, it is only to get what we want in a different way. Here, with U.G., all wanting beyond basic survival and procreation is wiped out. Other than the simple bodily necessities, wanting things from other people ceases. *All psychological and spiritual wants are without foundation.* This is U.G.'s disarming message: To seek through him any psychological satisfaction or any sort of spiritual gain, is to miss the point entirely.

For these reasons U.G. has *not* founded schools, ashramas, or meditation centers. He has no teaching to protect or disseminate. He has no following, gives no public talks, mounts no platforms, writes no strictures, offers no practice or *sadhana* of any kind, and offers no solutions to man's mounting problems. He is a private citizen, living in a house by the side of the road, talking informally with those who, for whatever reason, appear at his door. No one is asked to come and no one is asked to leave.

His life and teaching is writ on water, and the attempt by anyone to save, purify or institutionalize his message is a denial of all he is so fearlessly saying, and, therefore, absurd.

"I have no message for mankind," says U.G., "but of one thing I am certain, I cannot help you solve your basic dilemma or save you from self-deception, and *if I can't help you, no one can.*"

The editor hopes that this volume of conversations may serve, along with the first of U.G.'s books, "The Mystique of Enlightenment," to introduce readers to an uncommon man in an uncommon time, a man so ordinary and uncorrupted that he refused the exalted role of redeemer or world teacher, and instead points out, with indomitable courage and uncompromising integrity, the only real savior of man—that paradoxical freedom which is at once both uncomplaining self-reliance *and* unfrightened self-abandonment.

Terry Newland
Mill Valley, California
December, 1985

The Certainty *that* Blasts Everything

I can never sit on a platform and talk. It is too artificial. It is a waste of time to sit and discuss things in hypothetical or abstract terms. An angry man does not sit and talk and converse pleasantly about anger; he is too angry. So don't tell me that you are in crisis, that you are angry. Why talk of anger? You live and die in the hope that someday, somehow, you will no longer be angry. You are burdened with hope, and if this life seems hopeless, you invent the next life. There are no lives to come.

Well, it certainly cannot be said that your talking gives hope to anyone. Why do you talk if not to console or instruct?

What am I to do? You come, I talk. Do you want me to criticize you, to throw stones? It is useless, for you are affected by nothing, having erected an impenetrable armor around yourself. You feel nothing. Unable to understand your situation, you react through thought, which is your ideas and mentations. Reaction is thought. The pain you are going through there is clearly reflected without having to experience the pain here. Here there is no experience at all. That is all. In this natural state you feel the pain of others, whether you personally know them or not. Recently my eldest son was dying of cancer in a hospital nearby. I was in the area and visited him often. Friends said that I was in intense pain during the whole time, until he died. I cannot do anything. Pain is an expression of life. They wanted me to attempt some kind of healing for his cancer. If I touch that tumor it will grow, for I am adding life to it. Cancer is a multiplication of cells, another expression of life, and anything I might do only strengthens it.

So you can appreciate the suffering of others and yet are free of it yourself, is that it?

Suffering is an experience, and there is no experience here. You are not one thing, and life another. It is one unitary movement and anything I say about it is misleading, confusing. You are not a "person," not a "thing," not a discrete entity surrounded by "other" things. The unitary movement is not something which you can experience.

But to talk of living without experiencing sounds irrational to our minds.

What I am saying conflicts with your logical framework. You are using logic to continue that separative structure, that is all. Your questions are again thoughts and therefore reactive. All thought is reactive. You are desperately protecting this armor, this shield of thought, and are frightened that the movement of life might smash your frontiers. Life is like a river in spate, lashing at the banks, threatening the limits that have been placed around it. Your thought structure and your actual physiological framework are limited, but life itself is not. That is why life in freedom is painful to the body; the tremendous outburst of energy that takes place here is a painful thing to the body, blasting every cell as it goes. You cannot imagine how it is in your wildest dreams. This is why it is misleading no matter how I put it.

The gurus and priests teach us also that there is no separative structure and that that is the source of our problems. How do you differ from them?

For you, and them, it is just words. Your belief in a unitary movement of life is just a groundless belief, lacking any certainty. You have cleverly rationalized what the gurus and holy books have taught you. Your beliefs are the result of blind acceptance of authority, all secondhand stuff. You are not separate from your beliefs. When your precious beliefs and illusions come to an end, you come to an end. My talking is nothing more than the response to your pain, which you are expressing through questions, logical arguments, and other mentations.

But surely your sitting here and talking hour after hour indicates that you have a philosophy, a message to give, even if it is poorly understood by your listeners.

Not at all. There is nobody here talking, giving advice, feeling pain, or experiencing anything at all. Like a ball thrown against the wall, it bounces back, that is all. My talking is the direct result of your question; I have nothing here of my own, no obvious or hidden agenda, no product to sell, no axe to grind, nothing to prove.

But the body is transient, and we all aspire for some kind of immortality. Naturally we turn to higher philosophy, religion, the spiritual.

It is the body which is immortal. It only changes its form after clinical death, remaining within the flow of life in new shapes.

The body is not concerned with "the afterlife" or any kind of permanency. It struggles to survive and multiply *now*. The fictitious "beyond," created by thought out of fear, is really the demand for more of the same, in modified form. This demand for repetition of the same thing over and over again is the demand for permanence. Such permanence is foreign to the body. Thought's demand for permanence is choking the body and distorting perception. Thought sees itself as not just the protector of its own continuity, but also of the body's continuity. Both are utterly false.

It seems that some sort of radical change must take place, but without the interference of will.

If it occurs through no volition of yours, then that is the end of it. You will have no way of stopping it, of changing the situation at all. You cannot but go through it. It does no good to question reality. Question, rather, your goals, your beliefs, and assumptions. It is from them, not reality, that you must be freed. These pointless questions you are asking will disappear with the automatic abandonment of your goals. They are interdependent. One can't exist without the other.

Such a prospect is just too much. We fear oblivion, utter destruction.

If you drown, you drown. You will not sink. But what good are my assurances to you? Worthless, I'm afraid. You will continue doing what you are doing; its meaninglessness does not even occur to you. I tell you, when you stop doing things out of hope and the desire for continuity, all you do along with it stops. You will stay afloat. But still the hope remains there: "There must be *some* way, perhaps I am not doing it the right way." In other words, we have to accept the absurdity of depending upon *anything*. We must face our helplessness.

We just cannot help feeling that there must be some solution for our problems.

Your problems continue because of the false solutions you have invented. If the answers are not there, the questions cannot be there. They are interdependent; your problems and solutions go together. Because you want to use certain answers to end your problems, those problems continue. The numerous solutions offered by all these holy people, the psychologists, the politicians, are not really solutions at all. That is obvious. If there were legitimate answers, there would be no problems. They can only exhort you to try harder, practice more meditations, cultivate humility, stand on your head, and more and more of the same. That is all they can do. The teacher, guru, or leader who offers solutions is also false, along with his so-called answers. He is not doing any honest work, only selling a cheap, shoddy commodity in the marketplace. If you brushed aside your hope, fear, and naïveté and treated these fellows like businessmen, you would see that they do not deliver the goods, and never will. But you go on and on buying these bogus wares offered up by the experts.

But the whole field is so complicated that it seems necessary for us to rely on those who have studied carefully and devoted their lives to self-realization and wisdom.

All their philosophies cannot compare to the native wisdom of the body itself. What they are calling mental activity, spiritual activity, emotional activity, and feelings are really all one unitary process. This body is highly intelligent and does not need these scientific or theological teachings to survive and procreate. Take away all your fancies about life, death, and freedom, and the body remains unscathed, functioning harmoniously. It does not need your or my help. You don't have to do a thing. You will never again ask stupid, idiotic questions about immortality, afterlives, or death. The body is immortal.

You have mercilessly cut off every possibility of rehabilitation, obliterating even the faint hope of escaping this unhappiness. There seems to be nothing left but self-destruction. Why not suicide?

If you commit suicide, it does not help the situation in any way. The moment after suicide the body begins to decay, returning back to other, differently organized forms of life, putting an end to nothing. *Life has no beginning and no end.* A dead and dying body feeds the hungry ants there in the grave, and rotting corpses give off soil-enriching chemicals, which in turn nourish other life forms. You cannot put an end to your life, it is impossible. The body is immortal and never asks silly questions like, "Is there immortality?" It knows that it will come to an end in that particular form, only to continue on in others. Questions about life after death are always asked out of fear.

Those leaders who would direct your "spiritual life" cannot be honest about these things, for they make a living out of fear, speculations about future life, and the "mystery" of death.

And as for you, the followers, you are not really interested in the future of man, only your own petty little destinies. It is just a ritual you go through, talking for hours and hours about mankind, compassion, and the rest. It is *you* that you are interested in, otherwise there would not be this childish interest in your future lives, and your imminent demise.

But for many of us life is a sacred thing. We struggle to protect our children, the environment, to avert another war.

You are all neurotic people. You talk against birth control, drone on and on about the preciousness of life, then bomb and massacre. It is too absurd. You are concerned with an unborn life while you are killing thousands and thousands of people by bombing, starvation, poverty, and terrorism. Your "concern" about life is only to make a political issue out of it. It is just an academic discussion. I am not interested in that.

Yes, but many of us see all this and nevertheless are interested in changing things. It is not just egoism on our parts.

Are you really interested? Are you interested in the future of mankind? Your expressions of anger, righteousness, and caring have no meaning to me. It is just a ritual. You sit and talk, that's all. You are not at all angry. If you were angry at this moment, you would not ask this question, even to yourself. You sit everlastingly talking of anger. The angry wouldn't talk about it. The body has already acted with regard to that anger by absorbing it. The anger is burnt, finished then and there. You don't do anything; the body just absorbs it. That is all. If all this is too much for you, if it depresses you, don't ever go to the holy men. Take pills, do anything, but don't expect the holy business to help you. It is a waste of time.

You make me want to just drop the whole thing, to renounce...

As long as you think you have something to renounce, you are lost. Not to think of money and the necessities of life is an illness. It is a perversion to deny yourself the basic needs of life. You think that through a self-imposed asceticism you will increase your awareness and then be able to use that awareness to be happy. No chance. You will be peaceful when all your ideas about awareness are dropped and you begin to function like a computer. You must be a machine, function automatically in this world, never questioning your actions before, while, or after they occur.

Are you denying the importance of yogic practices, religious renunciation, or the value of a moral upbringing? Man is more than a machine, surely.

All moral, spiritual, ethical values are false. The psychologists, searching for a pragmatic way out, are now at the end of their tethers, even turning to the spiritual people for answers. They are lost, and yet the answers must come from them, not from the encrusted, useless traditions of the holy business.

This makes us all so helpless. No wonder people have relied upon messiahs, mahatmas and prophets.

The so-called messiahs have left nothing but misery in this world. If a modern messiah came before you, he would be unable to help you at all. And if he can't help, no one can.

If an anointed person, a savior or sage for example, can't be of help, then perhaps it is as the scriptures say, we must "know the truth and the truth shall make us free."

Truth is a movement. You can't capture it, contain it, give expression to it, or use it to advance your interests. The moment you capture it, it ceases to be the truth. What is the truth for me is something that cannot, under any circumstances, be communicated to you. The certainty here cannot be transmitted to another. For this reason the whole guru business is absolute nonsense. This has always been the case, not just now. Your self-denial enriches the priests. You deny yourself your basic needs while that man travels in a Rolls Royce car, eating like a king, and being treated like a potentate. He, and the others in the holy business, thrive on the stupidity and credulity of others. The politicians, similarly, thrive on the gullibility of man. It is the same everywhere.

Your emphasis is always on the negative side, the classic "neti neti" approach. Are you not pointing out the necessity of dropping all excess baggage, including the scriptures, gurus, and authorities, if one is to find that state you indicate is our natural birthright?

No. Doing away with the gurus, temples, and holy books as a prescription for freedom is ridiculous. You search for answers only as remedies for your problems, to avoid pain. Everything that is born is painful. There is no use asking why it is so. It is so. You think that by renouncing gurus and authorities you will suffer some divine endurance; endurance of pain is not going to help you spiritually. There is no way.

But we know you to be more than a fatalist, a cynic. You are pointing out a different destiny for man, not just critiquing his present predicament, are you not?

There is a solution for your problems—death. That freedom you are interested in can come about only at the point of death. Everybody attains *moksha* eventually, for moksha always foreshadows death, and everyone dies.

But I infer you do not mean death in any poetic or fanciful sense. It is not psychological, romantic, or abstract death you are describing, but real, actual, physical death, is it not?

Yes, that is it. When you die the body is in a prostrate position, it stops functioning, and that is the end of it. But in this case the body somehow renewed itself. It happens daily as a matter of course now; the whole process took years to stabilize. For me life and death are one, not two separate things. Just let me warn you that if what you are aiming at—moksha—really happens, you will die. There will be a physical death, because there has to be a physical death to be in that state. It is like playing around with controlling your breath because you find it amusing. But if you hold the breath long enough, you choke to death.

So we must become aware of death, making it an object of our meditations, and treating it in such a romantic, mystical way. Is that it?

To describe that state as a meditative state full of awareness is romantic hogwash. Awareness! What a fantastic gimmick gurus use to fool themselves and others. You can't be aware of every step, you only become self-conscious and awkward if you do. I once knew a man who was a harbor pilot. He had been reading about "passive awareness" and attempted to put it into practice. He, for the first time, nearly wrecked the ship he was guiding. Walking is automatic, and if you try to be aware of every step, you will go crazy. So don't invent meditative steps. Things are bad enough. The meditative state is worse.

But you can't just brush aside everything you hold sacred?

Of course I can; it is all just romantic stuff. Any remedy I offered you would become part of your search; that is, more romantic stuff. That is why I never tire of saying that I have no wares to sell, much less offer you new and better methods whereby you can continue your search. I deny the validity of that search entirely. You will get nothing here. Try your luck elsewhere.

But surely you are human and want to be of service to mankind, even if only out of pity?

Who elected me the redeemer? You have numerous saints, prophets and saviors who wish to serve you. Why add one more? Jesus said, "Knock and it shall open. Come all ye unto me." For some reason I am not able to do it. We have covered a lot of ground. Perhaps it is better if we continue this conversation tomorrow.

Until tomorrow then.

Thank you.

• • • •

From what you said yesterday, it seems obvious that one must be perfectly sane to do what you have done, that is, die. When we left off yesterday you were saying that one has to actually die if one is to discover freedom or moksha. A radical step such as this cannot be taken by a romantic, neurotic person. It is the act of a person free from self-absorption, neurotic episodes, and self-pity. Is there any way to teach this? Can people be educated to be sane?

I don't believe in education. You can teach a technique—mathematics, auto mechanics, but not integrity. How can you teach them about non-greed and non-ambition in an insanely greedy and ambitious society? You will only succeed in making them more neurotic.

Look, you are a cheat. Your religious ambitions are just like the businessman's there. If you can't cheat there is something wrong. How do you think the rich man there got his great wealth? Through lectures about non-greed and selflessness? Not at all. He got it by cheating somebody. Society, which is immoral to begin with, says that cheating is immoral, and that non-cheating is moral. I don't see the difference. If you get caught they put you in jail. So your food and shelter are provided for. Why worry? It is the guilt you have that compels you to talk of non-greed while you continue on with your greedy life. Your non-greed is invented by thought to keep you from facing the fact that greed is all that is there. But you are not satisfied with what is so. If there were nothing more than that, what would you do? That is all that is there. You just have to live with it. You can't escape. All thought can do is repeat itself over and over again. That is all it can do. And anything repetitive is senile.

Meditation seems less repetitive, deeper than ordinary thought. Yet it is unsatisfying.

If your meditations, sadhanas, methods and techniques meant anything, you wouldn't be here asking these questions. They are all means for you to bring about change. I maintain that there is nothing to change or transform. You accept that there is something to change as an article of faith. You never question the existence of the one who is to be changed. The whole mystique of enlightenment is based upon the idea of transforming yourself.

I cannot convey or transmit my certainty that you and all the authorities down through the centuries are false. They and the spiritual goods they peddle are utterly false. Because I cannot communicate this certainty to you it would be useless and artificial for me to get up on a platform and hold forth. I prefer to talk informally; I just talk, "Nice meeting you."

Then why do you talk at all?

There is no particular charm in being antisocial. I don't give people what they want. When they realize they will not get what they want here, they invariably go away. As they are leaving for the last time I like to add the rider, "You won't get it anywhere."

When people come to talk they find themselves confronted with silence itself. That is why everybody who comes is automatically silent thereafter. If he cannot stand the silence and insists upon talking and discussing things, he will be forced to disagree and walk out. But if you stay long, you will be silenced, not because it is over-persuasive, more rational than you are, but because it is silence itself silencing that movement there.

That silence burns everything here. All experiences are burnt. That is why talking to people doesn't exhaust me. It is energy to me. That is why I can talk for the whole day without showing any fatigue. Talking with so many people over the years has had no impact upon me. All that I or they have said is burnt here, leaving no trace. This is not, unfortunately, the case with you.

How does intelligence fit into all this? You seem to indicate that there is a native intelligence that has nothing to do with the accumulation of knowledge and technique.

Accepting the limitations is intelligence. You are trying to free yourself from these natural limitations and that is the cause of your sorrow and pain. Your actions are such that one action limits the next action. Your action at this moment is limiting the next action. This action is a reaction. The question of freedom of action does not even arise. Therefore no fatalistic philosophy is needed. The word *"karma"* means an action without a reaction. Any action of yours limits the action that is to take place next.

Any action that takes place at the conscious level of your thinking existence is a reaction. Pure, spontaneous action free of all previous actions is meaningless. The one and only action is the response of this living organism to the stimuli around it. That stimulus-response process is a unitary phenomenon. There is no division between action and reaction except when thought interferes and artificially separates them. Otherwise it is an automatic, unitary process, and there is nothing you can do to stop it. There is no need to stop it.

Just as in reality there is no separation of action and reaction, so there is no room for the religious man in the natural scheme of things. The fresh movement of life threatens his source of power and prestige. Still, he does not want to retire. He must be thrown out. Religion is not a contractual arrangement, either public or private. It has nothing to do with the social structure or its management. Religious authority wants to continue its hold on the people, but religion is entirely an individual affair. The saints and saviors have only succeeded in setting you adrift in life with pain and misery and the restless feeling that there must be something more meaningful or interesting to do with one's life.

Existence is all that is important, not how to live. We have created the "how" to live, which in turn has created this dilemma for us. Your thinking has created problems—what to eat, wear, how to behave—the body doesn't care. I am simply pointing out the absurdity of this conversation. Once you get the hang of it, you just go. I have no message to give mankind.

We have set in motion irreversible forces. We have polluted the sky, the waters, everything. Nature's laws know no reward, only punishment. The reward is only that you are in harmony with nature. The whole problem started when man decided that the whole universe was created for his exclusive enjoyment. We have superimposed the notion of evolution and progress over nature. Our mind—and there are no individual minds, only *mind*—which is the accumulation of the totality of man's knowledge and experience, has created the notion of the psyche and evolution. Only technology progresses, while we as a race are moving closer to complete and total destruction of ourselves and the world. Everything in man's consciousness is pushing the whole world, which nature has so laboriously created, towards destruction. There has been no qualitative change in man's thinking; we feel about our neighbors just as the frightened cave man felt towards his. The only thing that has changed is our ability to destroy our neighbor and his property.

Violence is an integral part of the evolutionary process. That violence is essential for the survival of the living organism. You can't condemn the hydrogen bomb, for it is an extension of the policeman there and your desire to be protected. Where do you draw the line? You can't. We have no way of reversing the whole thing.

Humanitarians insist that man has a capacity for love, and that love may be the only solution to mutual destruction. Is there anything to this?

Love and hate are exactly the same. They have together resulted in massacre, murder, assassination, and wars. This is a matter of history, not my opinion. Buddhism has resulted in horrors in Japan. It is the same thing everywhere. All our political systems have come out of that religious thinking, whether of the East or of the West. In the light of these facts, how can you have any faith in religion? What is the good of reviving the whole past, the useless past? It is because your living has no meaning to you that you dwell on the past. You are not even drifting. You have no direction at all; you are just floating. Obviously there is no purpose to your life, otherwise you would not live in the past.

What has not helped you cannot help anybody. No matter what I am saying, you are the medium of expression. You have already captured what I am saying and are making of it a new ism, ideology, and means to attain something. What I am trying to say is that you must discover something for *yourself.* But do not be misled into thinking that what you find will be of use to society, that it can be used to change the world. You are finished with society, that is all.

That thing that has to be discovered each by himself is God or enlightenment, is it not?

No. God is the ultimate pleasure, uninterrupted happiness. No such thing exists. Your wanting something that does not exist is the root of your problem. Transformation, moksha, liberation, and all that stuff are just variations on the same theme: permanent happiness. The body cannot take that. The pleasure of sex, for instance, is by nature temporary. The body can't take uninterrupted pleasure for long, it would be destroyed. Wanting to impose a fictitious, permanent state of happiness on the body is a serious neurological problem.

But the religions warn against pleasure-seeking. Through prayer, meditation, and various practices one is encouraged to transcend mere pleasure.

They sell you spiritual morphine. You take that drug and go to sleep. Now the scientists have perfected pleasure drugs, it is much easier to take. It never strikes you that the enlightenment and God you are after is just the ultimate pleasure, a pleasure moreover, which you have invented to be free from the painful state you are always in. Your painful, neurotic state is caused by wanting two contradictory things at the same time.

But somehow you are free of all these contradictions, and, although you claim not to be in any sort of perpetual bliss, you seem to be fundamentally happy. How come your life took this course and not others?

If I narrate the story of my life, it is as if I am describing somebody else's life. There is no attachment, sentiment, or emotional content for me when I consider my life. You get the wrong impression if you think I harbor any private, precious thoughts or feelings regarding my past.

For the first time, a man has broken away from the religious background[4], and already his teachings are outmoded, outdated, and misleading. J.K. has chosen the psychological form of explanation, which is already passé. You cannot destroy J.K., but the framework of thought he has created is already outdated and useless. The problem is not psychological, but physiological. This body has not fundamentally changed for hundreds of thousands of years. Its propensity to follow leaders, to avoid solitude, to wage war, to join groups—all such traits are in the genetic make-up of mankind, part of his biological inheritance.

Leaving aside the question of whether evil or good is possible for an organism that is already genetically programmed to be brutal and warlike, do not the religious practices—meditation, yoga, humility, etc.—attempt to help man go beyond these biological limitations?

Meditation is itself an evil. That is why all the evil thoughts swell up when you try to meditate. Otherwise you have no reference point, no way of knowing if the thoughts are good or evil thoughts. Meditation is a battle, but you only experience more pain. I can assure you that not only is the goal of meditation and moksha put into you by our culture, but that ultimately you will get nothing but pain. You may experience some petty little mystical experiences, which are of no value to you or anyone.

But we are not interested in any such petty experiences, we want freedom.

What is the difference whether or not you find this freedom, this enlightenment? You will not be there to benefit from it. What possible good can this state do you? This state takes away *everything* you have. That is why they call it *jivanmukti*—living in liberation. While living, the body has died. Somehow the body, having gone through death, is kept alive. It is neither happiness nor unhappiness. There is no such thing as happiness. This you do not, cannot, want. What you want is everything, here you lose everything. You want everything, and that is not possible. The religions have promised you so much—roses, gardens—and you end up with only thorns.

But other teachers, like J. Krishnamurti, describe a journey of discovery, that through awareness and free inquiry one can find out...

There is no transformation, radical or otherwise. That buffoon[5] talking in the circus tent there offers you a journey of discovery. It is a bogus charter flight. There is no such journey. The Vedic stuff is no more helpful. It was invented by some acid-heads after drinking some soma juice. J.K. is more neurotic than the people who go to listen to him.

If you put no credence in the ancient religious teachings, then do you take modern psychology any the more seriously?

The whole field of psychology has misled the whole thinking of man for a hundred years and more. Freud is the stupendous fraud of the 20th century. J. Krishnamurti talks of a revolution in the psyche. *There is no psyche there.* Where is this mind which is to be magically transformed? J.K.'s disciples have come to the point where all they can do is to repeat meaningless phrases. They are shallow, empty people. The fact that J.K. can draw large crowds means nothing; snake charmers also draw big crowds. Anybody can draw crowds.

But you are using a similar approach.

Yes, I am using 80% of his words and phrases, the very phrases he has used over the years to condemn gurus, saints, and saviors like himself. He has it coming. One thing I have never said: he is not a man of character. He has great character, but I am not in the least interested in men of character. If he sees the mess he has created in his false role as world Messiah and dissolves the whole thing, I will be the first to salute him. But he is too old and senile to do it. His followers are appalled that I am giving him a dose of his own medicine. Do not compare what I am saying with what he, or other religious authorities, have said. If you give what I am saying any spiritual overtones, any religious flavor at all, you are missing the point. All this has to be dropped.

But still it seems to us that J. Krishnamurti, and perhaps a few others in history, have something to say. J. Krishnamurti appears to be what he claims he is, a free man.

He has something. I am fond of saying that he has *seen* the sugar cube, but has not *tasted* the sugar cube. Whether that man, myself, or any other person is free or not is not your problem; it is the shibboleth of escapist minds, an amusement invented to avoid the real issue, which is your unfreedom. You may be sure of one thing: he who says he is a free man is a phony. Of this you may be sure. The thing you have to be free of is the "freedom" discussed by that man and other teachers. You must be free from "the first and last freedom," and all the freedoms that come in between.

If the notion of a life of grace, peace, and freedom are just fictions invited to escape our universal shallowness, then why proceed at all? If there is no abiding, transcendent reality to which man may turn, then why should we carry on our existence? Is there only eating, sleeping, and breathing?

That is all that is there. Go. Look, I am only saying that you must go find out for yourself if there is anything behind these meaningless abstractions being thrown at you. They talk of sacred hearts, universal minds, over-souls, you know, all the abstract, mystical terms used to seduce gullible people. Life has to be described in pure and simple physical and physiological terms. It must be demystified and depsychologized. Don't talk of "higher centers" and *chakras*. It is not these but glands that control the human body. It is the glands that give the instructions for the functioning of this organism. In your case you have introduced an interloper—thought. In your natural state thought ceases to control anything; it comes into temporary function when a challenge is put before it, immediately falling into the background when it is no longer needed.

So then no matter what we do, we are functioning in an unnatural way, is that it?

That is why I am pointing these things out. Forget about the ideal society and the ideal human being. Just look at the way you are functioning. That is the important thing. What has prevented the organism from fully flowering into its own uniqueness is culture. It has placed the wrong thing—the ideal person—before man. The whole thing is born out of the divisive consciousness of mankind. It has brought us nothing but violence. That is why no two gurus or saviors ever agree. Each is intent upon preaching his own nonsense.

What is it that draws us to hear you? Why are we interested in what you have to say?

You come for the same reason you go to anyone for answers: you want to know. You believe that in knowing my story you will be able to duplicate what happened to me. You, having been brainwashed all your life, can only think in terms of imitation. You think that somehow you can repeat what happened to me, that is all. That is your motive for coming. It is not a new approach to that religious stuff. It is completely different.

It has absolutely nothing to do with all that romantic, spiritual, religious stuff, nothing. If you translate what I am saying into religious terms, you are missing the point entirely. Religion, God, Soul, Beatitudes, moksha, are all just words, ideas used to keep your psychological continuity intact. When these thoughts are not there, what is left is the simple, harmonious physical functioning of the organism. I am able to describe the way this organism is functioning because your question has created the challenge here. Your questions create the conditions necessary for this response to happen. So, it is describing itself, but that is not the way it is functioning. It functions in a state of *not knowing*. I *never* ask myself how I am functioning. I *never* question my actions, before, while, or after they occur. Does a computer ask how it is functioning?

But computers have no feeling, no psyche, no spiritual dimension. How can you compare...?

You can't fit me into that religious framework. Any attempt on your part to translate what I am saying into your religious framework is to miss the point. I am not one of your holy men who say, "I am hanging, so come hang with me." All that stuff is a form of madness.

What's so mad about wanting to find out about life and death?

Because just as that crazy woman there says she is not mad, you insist upon saying there is death, that you are going to die. Both are false. As far as being states of mind based upon reality, both are equally invalid.

I think I am beginning to understand you intellectually.

Isn't it a joke to tell me that you understand what I am telling you? You say that you at least understand me intellectually, as if there were some other way of understanding. Your intellectual understanding, in which you have a tremendous investment, has not done one damn thing for you so far. You persist in the cultivation of this intellectual understanding, knowing all the while that it has never helped you at all. *This is amazing.* When hoping and attempting to understand is not there, then life becomes meaningful. Life, your existence, has a tremendous living quality about it. All your notions about love, beatitude, infinite bliss, and peace only block this natural energy of existence. How can I make you understand that what I am describing has absolutely nothing to do with all that religious stuff? You see hundreds of bodies carried off in the van after death, and yet you can't possibly imagine your own death. It is impossible, for your own death cannot be experienced by you. It is really something. It is no good throwing all this junk at me. Whatever hits this is immediately burnt—that is the nature of the energy here.

The spiritual people are the most dishonest people. I am emphasizing that foundation upon which the whole of spirituality is built. I am emphasizing that. If *there is no spirit,* then the whole talk of spirituality is bosh and nonsense. You can't come into your own being until you are free from the whole thing surrounding the concept of "self." To be really on your own, the whole basis of spiritual life, which is erroneous, has to be destroyed. It does not mean that you become fanatical or violent, burning down temples, tearing down the idols, destroying the holy books, like a bunch of drunks. It is not that at all. It is a bonfire inside of you. Everything that mankind has thought and experienced must go. The incredible violence in the world today has been created by the Jesuses and Buddhas.

But surely the attempt to become civilized is an attempt to transcend the laws of the jungle.

It is the ones who believe in God, who preach peace and talk of love, who have created the human jungle. Compared to man's jungle, nature's jungle is simple and sensible! In nature animals don't kill their own kind. That is part of the beauty of nature.

In this regard man is worse than the other animals. The so-called "civilized" man kills for ideals and beliefs, while the animals kill only for survival.

Man has strong ideals and beliefs because he seeks truth, which the animals don't.

There is no such thing as truth. The only thing that is actually there is your "logically" ascertained premise, which you call "truth."

But, again, all the great teachings have stressed the importance of finding truth through practice, selflessness and renunciation.

I renounce the only thing worth renouncing—the idea that there is renunciation at all. There is nothing to renounce. Your mistaken ideas regarding renunciation only create more fantasies about "truth," "God," etc.

It is not at all flattering to think that we are worse than other animals.

Because man is worse than the animals it made it necessary and possible for him to create the moral dilemma. When man first experienced the division in his consciousness—when he experienced his self-consciousness—he felt superior to other animals, which he is not, and therein sowed the seeds of his own destruction.

So, if I understand you correctly, you are saying that because we have falsely divided life into self and not-self, we have created a moral problem within us and in all our relationships. So our basic difficulty is thinking.

You can't experience anything except through thought. You can't experience your own body except through the help of thought.

The sensory perceptions are there. Your thoughts give form and definition to the body, otherwise you have no way of experiencing it. The body does not exist except as a thought. There is one thought. Everything exists in relationship to that one thought. That thought is "me." Anything you experience based on thought is an illusion.

Do not illusions persist only because awareness is not developed in us?

The word "awareness" is misleading. Awareness is not a divided state; there are not two states—awareness and something else. There are not two things. It is not that you are aware of something. Awareness is simply the action of the brain. The idea that you can *use* awareness to bring about some happier state of affairs, some sort of transformation, or God knows what, is, for me, absurd. Awareness cannot be used to bring about a change in yourself or the world around you.

All this rubbish about the conscious and the unconscious, awareness, and the self, is all a product of modern psychology. The idea that you can use awareness to get somewhere psychologically is very damaging. After more than a hundred years we seem unable to free ourselves from the psychological rubbish—Freud and the whole gang. Just what exactly do you mean by consciousness? You are conscious, aware, only through thought. The other animals use thought—the dog, for example, can recognize its owner—in a simple manner. They recognize without using language. Humans have added to the structure of thought, making it much more complex. Thought is not yours or mine; it is our common inheritance. There is no such thing as your mind and my mind. There is only *mind*—the totality of all that has been known, felt, and experienced by man, handed down from generation to generation. We are all thinking and functioning in that "thought sphere," just as we all share the same atmosphere for breathing. The thoughts are there to function and communicate in this world sanely and intelligently.

Still, we actually feel that there is a thinker thinking these thoughts, sort of a "ghost in the machine," that thinking involves more than the mechanical response of memory.

The knowledge—that is all that is there. The "me," "psyche," "mind," "I," or whatever you want to call it is nothing else than the totality of the inherited knowledge passed on to us from generation to generation, mostly through education. You teach the child to distinguish between colors, to read, to imitate manners. It is relative to each culture: Americans learn American manners, Indians learn Indian manners, etc. Gestures of the body, of hands or of face constituted the first language. Later words were added on. We still use gestures to supplement our spoken words because we feel that words alone are inadequate to fully express what we want to convey.

All this is not to say that we can really know anything about thought. We can't. You become conscious of thought only when you make it an object of thought, otherwise you don't even know you are thinking. We use thought only to understand something out there, to remember something, or to achieve something. Otherwise we don't even know if thought is there or not. Thought is not separate from the movement of thought. Thought is action, and without it you cannot act. There is no such thing as pure, spontaneous, thought-free action at all. To act is to think.

You have a self-starting, self-perpetuating mechanism, which I call the self. This does not mean that there is actually an entity there. I do not want or mean to give that connotation to that word. Where is this ego, or self, that you talk of? Your non-existent self has heard of spirituality and bliss from someone. To experience this thing called bliss you feel you must control your thoughts. It is impossible, you will burn yourself and die if you attempt it.

Philosophers are often heard talking of a "now," independent of past and future. Is there such a thing as an eternal present?

The demand for more and more experience constitutes your "present," which is born out of the past. Look. Here is a microphone before you. You are looking at it. Is it possible for you to look at it without the word microphone? The instrument you are using to look at and experience the microphone is the past, your past. If that is seen there is no future at all. Any achievement you are interested in is in the future. The only way that the future can come into operation is in the present moment. Unfortunately, in the present moment what is in operation is the past. Your past is creating your future; in the past you were happy or unhappy, foolish or wise, in the future you will be the opposite. So the future can't be any the different from the past.

When the past is not in operation there is no present at all, for what you are calling the present is the past repeating itself. In an actual state of here and now there is no past in operation and, therefore, no future. I do not know if you are following me. The only way the past can survive and maintain its continuity is through the constant demand to experience the same thing over and over. That is why life has become a bore. Life has become boring because we have made of it a repetitive thing. So what we mistakenly call the present is really the repetitive past projecting a fictitious future. Your goals, your search, your aspirations are cast in that mold.

One problem with understanding the past is its ephemerality. The psyche or mind has to be located somewhere if, as you say, there is no soul and no higher planes. Where, if I can put it that way, is the past?

From your knowledge, out of the past, you ask questions, and the very motive of your asking is only to gain more knowledge from someone else, so that your knowledge structure can continue. You are really not interested in this at all. Your knowledge coming to an end means that *you* are coming to an end. Where, you ask, is this knowledge, the past? Is it in your brain? Where is it? It is all over your body. It is in every cell of your body.

These questions all spring from your search. It doesn't matter what the object of that search is—God, a beautiful woman or man, a new car. It is all the same search. And that *hunger will never be satisfied.* That hunger must burn itself out completely without knowing satisfaction. The thirst you have must burn itself out without being quenched. It dawns on you that this is not the way, and it is finished.

What I am emphasizing is that we are trying to solve our basic human problems through a psychological framework, when actually the problem is neurological. The body is involved. Take desire. As long as there is a living body, there will be desire. It is natural. Thought has interfered and tried to suppress, control, and moralize about desire, to the detriment of mankind. We are trying to solve the "problem" of desire through thought. It is thinking that has created the problem. You somehow continue to hope and believe that the same instrument can solve your other problems as well. You hope against hope that thought will pull you through, but you will die in hope just as you have lived in hope. That is the refrain of my doom song.

All religions have placed the desire for freedom, heaven, liberation, or God before all others as being worthy of pursuit. But if these ultimate goals do not exist, as you seem to suggest, they are, therefore, inferior desires, being false and hence impossible to satisfy. But this repels us; we insist that some desires, especially those which ostensibly transcend "the flesh," are more divine than others. Would you comment on this?

Unless you are free from the desire of all desires, moksha, liberation, or self-realization, you will be miserable. The ultimate goal—which society has placed before us—is the one that has to go. Until you are free from that desire, you cannot be free from any of your miseries. By suppressing these desires, you are not going to be free. This realization is the essential thing, going as it does to the crux of the problem. It is society that has placed the desire for freedom, the desire for liberation, the desire for

God, the desire for moksha—that is the desire you must be free from. Then all these other desires fall into their own natural rhythm. You suppress these desires only because you are afraid society will punish you if you act on them, or because you see them as "obstacles" to your main desire—freedom.

If this kind of thing should happen to you, you will find yourself back in a primeval state without primitivity, and without any volition on your part. It just happens. Such a free man is not in conflict with society any more. He is not antisocial, not at war with the world; he sees that it can't be any the different. He doesn't want to change society at all; the demand for change has ceased. Any doing in any direction is violence. Any effort is violence. Anything you do with thought to create a peaceful state of mind is using force, and so, is violent. Such an approach is absurd. You are trying to enforce peace through violence. Yoga, meditations, prayers, *mantras,* are all violent techniques. The living organism is *very* peaceful; you don't have to do a thing. The peacefully functioning body doesn't care one hoot for your ecstasies, beatitudes, or blissful states.

Man has abandoned the natural intelligence of the body. That is why I say—it is my "doom song"—that the day man experienced that consciousness that made him feel separate and superior to the other animals, at that moment he began sowing the seeds of his own destruction. This warped view of life is slowly pushing the entire thinking towards total annihilation. There is nothing you can do to halt it.

I am not an alarmist. I am not frightened, I am not interested in saving the world. Mankind is doomed anyway.

All I am saying is that the peace you are seeking is already inside you, in the harmonious functioning of the body.

It sounds more and more like the joke about the Buddha saying, "Don't just do something, stand there." Not making movement in any direction at any level is not so easy.

Anything you do to free yourself from anything for whatever

reason is destroying the sensitivity, clarity, and freedom that is already there.

If it were possible to see things as they really are...

There is no question of your seeing things as they are. You can't see things as they are. You never leave any experience or feeling you have alone. You have to capture and interpret that feeling within the framework of the known. You are happy or unhappy only as you have knowledge about and experience of happiness and unhappiness. So everything has to be brought within the framework of the known before you can experience it. The movement of the known is gathering momentum within you. Its only interest is to continue. There is no entity, no self there to give itself continuity; it is just the movement of thought, the self-perpetuating separation. It is mechanical. Anything you try to do about it only adds momentum to it.

Eastern teachers have said that desire is an evil, that it must be transcended.

It is the desire to reach a particular goal, an all important goal, that must go, not the countless petty little desires. The only reason you try to manipulate or control the petty desires is that such control is a part of your strategy to attain the highest goal, the desire of all desires. Eliminate that main goal and the others fall into a natural pattern and pose no problem for you or for the world. You won't get anywhere by trying to endlessly control and manipulate these numerous desires. It is vicious in its nature.

Is there any higher goal at all?

The so-called "highest goal" is like the horizon. The further you move towards it, the further it recedes. The goal, like the horizon, is not really there. It is a projection of your own fear and it moves away from you as you pursue it. How can you keep up with it? There is nothing that you can do. Still, it is desire that keeps you moving; no matter in which direction you move, it is the same.

You say that I am living in illusion. But poverty, work, war, they are not illusions. Are they? In what sense am I being deluded?

What you experience through your separative consciousness is an illusion. You can't say that falling bombs are an illusion. It is not an illusion, only your experience of it is an illusion. The reality of the world that you are experiencing now is an illusion. That is all I am trying to say.

If you say that my relative, subjective world view is biased and therefore illusory, I am prepared to agree with you. But you also deny any outside, objective measure of absolute reality, do you not?

There is no such thing as absolute. It is thought, and thought alone, that has created the absolute. Absolute zero, absolute power, absolute perfection, these have been invented by the holy men and "experts." They kidded themselves and others.

Down the centuries the saints, saviors, and prophets of mankind have kidded themselves and everybody else. Perfection and absolutes are false. You are trying to imitate and relate your behavior according to these absolutes, and it is falsifying you. You are actually functioning in an entirely different way; you are brutal, you feel you must be peaceful. It is contradictory, that's all I'm pointing out.

We wonder at your eagerness to deny all the religious and philosophical authorities.

The certainty that dawned upon me is something which cannot be transmitted. It does not mean that I am superior, a chosen one, one in whom all the virtues are rolled into one. Not at all.

I am just an ordinary man and have nothing to do with it. This certainly blasts everything, including the claims of the so-called enlightened ones selling things in the marketplace.

If the holy men and saviors have been wrong about man's proper place in the scheme of things, surely they have been at least partially right in pointing towards a higher unity, God, if you will.

What I am trying to put across is that there is no such thing as God. It is the mind that has created God out of fear. Fear is passed on from generation to generation. *What is there is fear, not God.* If you are lucky enough to be free from fear, then there is no God. There is no ultimate reality, no God—nothing. Fear itself is the problem, not "God." Wanting to be free from fear is itself fear.

You see, you love fear. The ending of fear is death, and you don't want *that* to happen. I am not talking of wiping out the phobias of the body. They are necessary for survival. The death of fear is the only death.

Until we somehow find the courage to die to our fears we continue to...

...hope, pray, practice virtues. The man who practices virtue is a man of vice. Only such a man, a man of vice, would practice virtue. There is not a virtuous man in the world. All men will be virtuous *tomorrow,* until then they remain men of vice. Your virtue only exists in the fictitious future. Where is this virtue you are talking of? It is no good hoping to be virtuous in a future life either; there is no guarantee that there is any future life, much less that you will be free in it.

I think I am beginning to see what...

You are blind. You see nothing. When you actually do see and perceive for the first time that there is no self to realize, no psyche to purify, no soul to liberate, it will come as a tremendous shock to that instrument. You have invested everything in that—the soul, mind, psyche, whatever you wish to call it—and suddenly it is exploded as a myth. It is difficult for you to look at reality, at your actual situation. One look does the trick; you are finished.

It is radical, and perhaps a little dangerous, to call the spirit, the soul, and God the shoddy inventions of frightened minds, is it not?

I don't care. I am ready to go. I don't see anything other than the physical activity of the body. Spirituality is the invention of the mind, and the *mind is a myth.*

Your traditions are choking you. But, unfortunately, you don't do anything. You actually love being choked. You love the burden of the cultural garbage-sack, the dead refuse of the past. It has to drop away naturally. It just drops. You don't depend upon knowledge anymore, except as a useful tool to function sanely in this world.

Wanting has to go. Wanting to be free from something that is not there is what you call "sorrow." Wanting to be free from sorrow is sorrow. There is no other sorrow. You don't want to be free from sorrow. You just think about sorrow, without acting. Your thinking endlessly about being free from sorrow is only more material for sorrow. Thinking does not put an end to sorrow. Sorrow is there for you as long as you think. There is actually no sorrow there to be free from. Thinking about and struggling against "sorrow" is sorrow. Since you can't stop thinking, and thinking is sorrow, you will always suffer. There is no way out, no escape.

Hope Is
for Tomorrow,
Not Today

I *would like to be able to meditate and have real peace of mind.*

Have you questioned this goal of yours, which makes sadhana necessary? Why take it for granted that there is such a thing as "peace of mind?" Maybe it is a false thing. I am just asking the question to understand what particular goal you have. May I ask that question?

As I said, I would like to have peace of mind.

When do you expect to have it? It is always tomorrow, next year. Why? Why does tranquility, or quietness of the mind, or whatever you choose to call it, only happen tomorrow—why not now? Perhaps this disturbance—this absence of tranquility—is caused by the very sadhana itself.

It must *be possible.*

But why are you putting it off until tomorrow? You have to face the situation *now*. What ultimately do you want?

Whatever I do seems meaningless. There is no sense of satisfaction. I feel that there must be something higher than this.

Suppose I say that this meaninglessness is all there is for you, all there can ever be for you. What will you do? The false and absurd goal you have before you is responsible for that dissatisfaction and meaninglessness in you. Do you think life has any meaning? Obviously you don't. You have been told that there *is* meaning, that there *must* be a meaning to life. Your notion of the "meaningful" keeps you from facing this issue, and makes you feel that life has no meaning. If the idea of the meaningful is dropped, then you will see meaning in whatever you are doing in daily life.

But we all have to have an idea of a better, more spiritual life.

Whatever you want, even the so-called spiritual goals, is materialistic in value. What, if I may ask, is so spiritual about it? If you want to achieve a spiritual goal, the instrument you use will be the same which you use to achieve materialistic goals, namely *thought*. You don't actually do anything about it; you just think. So you are just thinking that there must be some purpose to life. And because thought is matter, its object—the spiritual or meaningful life-is also matter. Spirituality is materialism. In any event you do not *act,* you just think, which is to postpone. There is simply nothing else thought can do.

That instrument called thought, which you are employing to achieve your so-called spiritual goals, is the result of the past. Thought is born in time, it functions in time, and any results it seeks are bound to be in and of time also. And time is postponement, the tomorrow. Take, for example, the fact of selfishness. It is condemned, while selflessness, a pure creation of thinking, is to be sought after. Its realization, however, lies always just ahead, tomorrow. You will be selfless tomorrow, or the next day, or, if there is one, in the next life. Why is it not possible for you to be totally free from selfishness now, today? And do you really want to be free from selfishness? You do not, and that is why you have invented what you call selflessness, in the meantime remaining selfish. So, you are not going to be selfless at all, ever, because the instrument which you use to achieve that state of selflessness or peace of mind is materialistic in value. Whatever you do to be free from selfishness will only strengthen and fortify it. I am not saying that you should therefore be selfish, only that thinking about its abstract opposite, which you have called "selflessness," is useless.

You have also been told that through meditation you can bring selfishness to an end. Actually, you are not meditating at all, just thinking about selflessness, and doing nothing to be selfless. I have taken that as an example, but all other examples are variations of the same thing. All activity along these lines is exactly the same. You must accept the simple fact that you do not want to be free from selfishness.

I am making an effort to understand.

You are using effort to be in an effortless state. How the hell can you use effort to be in an effortless state? You think that you can live an effortless life through volition, struggle, and effort. Unfortunately, that is all you can do. Effort is all you know. The "you," and everything it has achieved, has been a result of effort. Effortlessness through effort is like peace through war. How can you have peace through war?

The "peace of mind" you want is an extension of this war of effort and struggle. So is meditation warfare. You sit for meditation while there is a battle raging within you. The result is violent, evil thoughts welling up inside you. Next, you try to control or direct these brutal thoughts, making more effort and violence for yourself in the process.

But there does seem to be something like peace of mind when one finishes one's prayers or meditations. How do you explain that?

It is the result of sheer exhaustion, that's all. Your attempts to control or suppress your thoughts only tire you out, making you sort of battle-weary. That is the effortlessness and peace of mind you are experiencing. It is not peace. If you want techniques for thought control, you have come to the wrong man.

No sir, I feel that I am benefited by talking with you. Are you saying that no religious commitment, no spiritual path, no sadhana is necessary?

I say no. Somebody else says yes. Where does that leave you? Understanding your goal is the main thing. To achieve that goal implies struggle, battle, effort, will, that is all. There is no guarantee that you will reach your goal. You *assume* the goal is there. You have invented the goal to give yourself *hope*. But hope means tomorrow. Hope is necessary for tomorrow, not for today.

You know. You want more knowledge so you can develop better techniques for reaching your goal. You know that there is no guarantee that more experience, more knowledge, more systems and more methods will help you reach your goal. Yet you persist; it is all you know how to do. Seeing today demands action. Seeing tomorrow involves only hope.

What is it that we are trying to see with the help of techniques?

You want to see meaning in your life. As long as you persist in searching for a purpose or meaning to life, so long whatever you are doing will seem purposeless and meaningless. The hope you have of finding meaning is what is causing the present state of meaninglessness. There may not be any meaning other than this.

It is understandable that people should look for meaning in their lives, isn't it?

The energy you are devoting to the search, to techniques, to your sadhana, or whatever you wish to call it, is taking away the energy you need to live. You are obsessed with finding meaning in life, and that is consuming a lot of energy. If that energy is released from the search for meaning, it can be used to see the futility of all search. Then your life becomes meaningful and the energy may be used for some useful purpose. Life, the so-called material life, has a meaning of its own. But you have been told that it is devoid of meaning and have superimposed a fictitious layer of "spiritual" meaning over it.

Why should life have any meaning? Why should there be any purpose to living? Living itself is all that is there. Your search for spiritual meaning has made a problem out of living. You have been fed all this rubbish about the ideal, perfect, peaceful, purposeful way of life, and you devote your energies to thinking about that rather than living fully. In any case you are living, no matter what you are thinking about. Life has to go on.

But isn't that the goal of culture and education, to teach us how to live?

You are living. As soon as you introduce the question "how to live?" you have made of life a problem. "How" to live has made life meaningless. The moment you ask "how," you turn to someone for answers, becoming dependent.

You are saying that all search is doomed because there is nothing to achieve or understand.

There is nothing to be achieved, nothing to accomplish. Because you have created the goal—say, selflessness—you remain stuck in selfishness. If the goal of selflessness is not there, are you selfish? You have invented selflessness as an object to pursue, meanwhile continuing to be selfish. How can you ever end your selfishness as long as you pursue selflessness? A certain amount of practical selfishness is necessary for survival, of course, but with you it has become a tremendous, unsolvable problem.

Here there is no need to sit in special postures and control your breath. Even while my eyes are open, in fact no matter what I am doing, I am in a state of *samadhi*. The knowledge you have about samadhi is what is keeping you away from it. Samadhi comes after the ending of all you have ever known, at death. The body has to become like a corpse before that knowledge, which is locked into every cell in the body, ceases.

You infer that a complete radical break with one's past is essential if one is to get beyond the prevalent mediocrity, if one is to live creatively. But there have been a great many intelligent, inventive people who have not undergone any death process or physiological "calamity," as you call it.

Your highly praised inventiveness springs from your thinking, which is essentially a protective mechanism. The mind has invented both religion and dynamite to protect what it regards as its best interests. There is no good or bad in this sense. Don't you see? All these bad, brutal, terrible people, who should have been eliminated long ago, are thriving and successful. Don't think that you can get off this merry-go-round, or that by pretending to be spiritually superior you are avoiding any complicity. You are the world; you are *that*. This is all I am pointing out.

Are you also brushing aside the concern for what might happen to one in a future life? If, in a later life, I shall reap what I have sown, should I not be concerned with how to be moral?

Past lives, future lives, karma—these things are emphasized in this so-called "spiritual" country. It is a total failure! They say that they will have to suffer for their bad actions in the future, tomorrow. But what about now? Why is he getting away with it now? Why is he so successful right now?

Despite the obvious chaos and brutality in the world, most of us find that hope springs eternal and that love must ultimately rule the world.

There is no love in the world. Everybody wants the same thing. Whosoever is the most ruthless gets it—as long as he can get away with it. Getting what you want in this world is a relatively easy thing, if you are ruthless enough. I had everything a man could want, every kind of desirable experience, and it all failed me. Therefore, I can never recommend my "path" to anyone, having eventually faced the falseness of that path myself and rejected it. I would never even hint that there was any validity in all those experiences and practices.

Contrary to what you have said, the great saviors and leaders of mankind have agreed that...

The saints, saviors, priests, gurus, *bhagavans,* seers, prophets and philosophers were all wrong, as far as I am concerned. As long as you harbor any hope or faith in these authorities, living or dead, so long this certainty cannot be transmitted to you. This certainty somehow dawns on you when you see for yourself that all of them are wrong.

When you see all this for yourself for the first time, you explode. That explosion hits life at a point that has never been touched before. It is absolutely unique. So whatever I may be saying cannot be true for you. The moment you see it for yourself you make what I am saying obsolete and false. All that came before is negated in that fire. You can't come into your own uniqueness unless the whole of human experience is thrown out of your system. It cannot be done through any volition or the help of anything. Then you are on your own.

It seems to me that a special sort of valor is necessary for what you are describing. Am I right?

Yes. But it is not courage in the usual sense. It is not the courage you associate with struggle or overcoming. The valor I am talking about is the courage that is naturally there when all this authority and fear is thrown out of the system. Courage is not an instrument or quality you can use to get somewhere. The stopping of doing is courage. The ending of tradition in you is courage.

Even with courage there is no guarantee that one isn't wrong about life, or that one is not mistaken about the important things.

When once you are freed from the pairs of opposites—right and wrong, good and bad—you will never be wrong. But until then the problem will be there.

Reaching the end of opposites has rather frightening implications.

It is like accidentally touching a live wire. You are much too frightened to touch it through your own volition. By sheer accident this thing touches you, burning everything.

Including the search for God and freedom?

It burns out this search, the hunger. The hunger stops, not because it is satisfied. The hunger can never be satiated, especially by the traditional food that is offered. With the burning away of that hunger, the duality ceases. That is all.

There is a certain uneasiness when listening to you.

You are incapable of listening to anyone. You are the medium of my expression. I respond to your questions; I have nothing of my own. The expression of what is here occurs because of you, not me. That medium—you—is corrupt. The medium is only interested in maintaining its own continuity. So anything that happens there is already dead.

You seem bent upon demolishing everything other teachers have taught.

My interest is not to knock off what others have said (that is too easy), but to knock off what *I* am saying. More precisely, I am trying to stop what you are making out of what I am saying. This is why my talking sounds contradictory to others. I am forced by the nature of your listening to always negate the first statement with another statement. Then the second statement is negated by a third, and so on. My aim is not some comfy dialectical thesis, but the total negation of everything that can be expressed. Anything you try to make out of my statements is not it.

You sense a freshness, a living quality to what is being said here. That is so, but this cannot be used for anything. It cannot be repeated. It is worthless. All you can do with it is to try to organize it—create organizations, open schools, publish holy books, celebrate birthdays, sanctify holy temples, and the like, thus destroying any life it may have had in it. No individual can be helped by such things. They only help those who would live by the gullibility of others.

How exactly did the system free itself from tradition in your case?

My explanation is that there was an outburst of energy, which is utterly different from the energy that is born out of thinking. All spiritual, mystical experiences are born out of thought. They are thought-induced states, nothing more. The energy here that is burning all thought as it arises tends to accumulate. Eventually it has to escape. The physical limitations of the body act as obstacles to the escape of this unique energy. When it escapes it goes up, never down, and never returns. When this extraordinary energy—which is atomic—escapes, it causes tremendous pain. It is not the pain you are familiar with. It has nothing to do with it. If it did, the body would be shattered. It is not matter converting into energy; it is atomic. The process goes on and on, while the pain comes and goes. It is like the tremendous relief when a tooth is extracted. That is the kind of relief that is there, not the spiritual. The translation of this as bliss or beatitude is very misleading. Through thought anyone can create those experiences; but it is not actually bliss. The real thing is not something that can be experienced. Anything you can experience is old. That means everything you experience or understand is tradition.

In other words, I am trying to free you not from the past, the conditioning, but, rather, from what I am saying. I am not suggesting any way out because there is no way. I have stumbled into this and freed myself from the paths of others. I can't make the same mistake they did. I will never suggest that anyone use me as a model or follow in my footsteps. My path can never be your path. If you attempt to make this your path, you will get caught in a rut. No matter how refreshing, revolutionary or fantastic, it is still a rut, a copy, a secondhand thing. I myself do not know how I stumbled into this, so how do you expect me to give it to another?

My mission, if there is any, should be, from now on, to debunk every statement I have made. If you take seriously and try to use or apply what I have said, you will be in danger.

Great teachers and seers in the Eastern tradition have at least attempted to convey some idea of higher states, while you insist they are incommunicable. Why?

You take for granted that they are what they say they are. I say it cannot be transmitted to another because there is nothing there to transmit. Neither is there anything to renounce. What is it that these teachers suggest you should renounce? Even your scriptures—the Kathopanishad—say that you must renounce the very search itself. The renunciation of renunciation happens not through practice, discussion, money, or intellect. These are the least of things. A rough translation of the original *Sanskrit* is, "Whomsoever it chooses, to him it is revealed." If this is so, then where is the room for practices, sadhana, and volition? It comes randomly, not because you deserve it.

If you are lucky enough to have this dawn on you, you will die. It is the continuity of thought that dies. The body has no death, it only changes form. The ending of thought is the beginning of physical death. What you experience is the emptiness of the void. But there is no death for the body at all. I am sure this is of little consolation to you, though. Just wanting to be free of egoism is insufficient; you must go through a clinical death to be free from thought and egoism. The body will actually get stiff, the heartbeat slows, and you will become corpse-like.

The theory of reincarnation also denies death, but in a different way. They speak of an eternal atma *or soul which outlives the physical death...*

Whatever answers are given regarding death, you are not satisfied with them, and so you must invent theories about reincarnation. What is it that will reincarnate? Even while you are alive, what is there? Is there anything beyond the totality of the knowledge which exists inside you now? So, is there death at all, and if there is, can it be experienced?

So you will only confirm the existence of a natural state, is that it?

The ideas you have about that natural state are totally unrelated to what it actually is. You are trying to capture and give expression to what you hope is that state. It is an absurd exercise. What is there is only the movement to capture, nothing else. All the rest is speculation.

Not Knowing Is Your Natural State

From our earlier talks with you it is evident that man has a wrong relationship with his knowledge of himself and the world. What exactly do you mean by knowledge?

Knowledge is not something mysterious or abstract. I look at the table and ask myself, "What is that?" So do you. Knowledge is just naming things. It tells you that that is a "table," that I "am happy" or "miserable," that "you are an enlightened man and I am not." Is there anything to thought other than this?

The knowledge you have of the world creates the objects you are experiencing. The actual existence or non-existence of something "out there" in the world is not something you can determine or experience for yourself, except through the help of your knowledge. And this knowledge is not yours; it is something which you and your ancestors have accumulated over a long time. What you call the "act of knowing" is nothing other than this accumulated memory. You have personally added to and modified that knowledge, but essentially it doesn't belong to you at all.

There is nothing there inside you but the totality of this knowledge you have accumulated. That is what you are. You cannot even directly experience the reality of the world in which you are functioning, much less some world beyond. There is no world beyond space and time. It is your invention, based upon the vague promises of the holy men. Our sense of value springs from the world as it is imposed on us. We must accept the world.

So our belief system is also based upon this memory?

Neither is belief an abstraction. It is an extension of the survival mechanism which has operated for millions of years. Belief is like any other habit, the more you try to control and suppress it, the stronger it becomes. Your question implies that you want to be free from something—in this case it is belief. First of all, why do you want to be free from it? Whatever you are doing or hope to do to be free from this only adds momentum to it. Anything you do has no value at all. Why has this become a problem to you? You are in no position to deny or accept what I am saying. You have probably tried some kind of system to control your thoughts and beliefs, and it has failed you. Repeating mantras, doing yoga, and prayer have not helped. For whatever reasons, you have not been able to control your thoughts. That is all.

But the repeating of mantras and other sacred techniques do seem to quiet thought.

You cannot even observe your thoughts, much less control them. How can you possibly observe your thoughts? You talk as though there is some entity in you separate from thoughts. It is an illusion; your thoughts are *not* separate from you. There is no thinking. Thought cannot damage you. It is your separative structure trying to control, dominate, censure and use thought that is the problem. *Thought by itself can do no damage.* It is only when you want to do something with thought that you create problems for yourself.

Listening to you now seems also to create problems for me.

You say you are listening. Even as I speak you are not listening to anything. You are not listening to me, but only to your own thoughts. I have no illusions about it. You *cannot* listen to me or anybody. It is useless trying to persuade me that you are attentive, concerned, listening. I am not a fool.

It is not so obvious to me that I am not listening to you. I seem to be listening to you and thinking about it simultaneously. Isn't this possible?

It is impossible. There is only one action possible for you: thinking. The birth of thought itself is action. The thinker who says he is looking at cause-and-effect is himself thought. Thought creates the space between the thinker and his thoughts, and then tells himself, "I am looking at my thoughts." Is it possible? Forgetting about what has happened in the past, try to look at your thoughts at this very moment. I am asking you to do something which is quite simple. If you will tell me how to look at thought, I will be your student. I will be very grateful to you. Instead of looking at thought, you focus on me. If you repeat a mantra, that is thought. The repetition of the mantra is another thought. The idea that these repetitive thoughts have not succeeded in producing the state you want is another thought. The idea that you must find a new mantra or practice some technique that *does* work is another thought. What is thought other than this? I want to know.

But all religions have stressed the importance of suppressing and controlling undesirable thoughts. Otherwise we would descend to the level of animals.

We have been brainwashed for centuries by holy men that we must control our thoughts. Without thinking you would become a corpse. Without thinking the holy men wouldn't have any means of telling us to control our thoughts. They would go broke. They have become rich telling others to control their thoughts.

But, surely, there are qualitative differences in the way thoughts are controlled.

You have arbitrarily made these distinctions. Thinking is part of life, and life is energy. Having a glass of beer or smoking a cigarette is exactly the same as repeating prayers, holy words, and scriptures. Going to the pub or the temple is exactly the same; it is a quick fix. You attach special significance to the prayers and temples, for no reason other than that it is your prejudice and that it makes you feel superior to those who frequent pubs and bordellos.

So it is all an attempt to modify or change in some way my conditioning.

Conditioning is tradition. The Sanskrit word for it is *samskara*. Tradition is what you are—what you call *you*. No matter how you may modify it, it continues. In life everything is temporary, and the attempt to give continuity to conditioning—which is based upon thought—is pathological in nature. You treat the psychological and the pathological as if they were two different things. Actually there is only the pathological there. Your samskara, the conditioning that makes you feel separate from yourself and the world, is pathological.

Where is this conditioning you talk of? Where are the thoughts located? They are not in the brain. Thoughts are not manufactured by the brain. It is, rather, that the brain is like an antenna, picking up thoughts on a common wavelength, a common thought-sphere.

All your actions, whether thinking of God or beating a child, spring from the same source—thinking. The thoughts themselves cannot do any harm. It is when you attempt to use, censor, and control those thoughts to *get* something that your problems begin. You have no recourse but to use thought to get what you want in this world. But when you seek to get what does not exist—God, bliss, love, etc.—through thought, you only succeed in pitting one thought against another, creating misery for yourself and the world.

When the thought structure, pressed into the service of fear and hope, cannot achieve what it wants, or cannot be certain, it introduces what you call "faith." Where is the need for belief, or its alter-ego faith? When your beliefs have gotten you nowhere, you are told you must cultivate faith. In other words, you must have hope. Whether you are seeking God, or bliss, peace of mind, or, more tangibly, happiness, you end up relying on hope, belief, and faith. These dependencies are the tokens of your failure to get the results you desire.

What is the relationship between thought conditioning, and what we call desire?

Your desires, like your thoughts in general, are to be suppressed and controlled at all costs. This approach only enriches the holy men. Why the hell do you want to be in what you call "a desireless state" anyhow? What for? I can assure you that when you have no desire you will be carried as a corpse to the burial ground.

We have been told by the holy men that to have desires is wrong. They must be suppressed or changed into a higher order of desires, "transformed." It is hogwash. Either you fulfill those desires or you fail to fulfill those desires. That is the problem. In either case desire will arise. Attempting to do nothing is also useless. It is part of your general strategy to get something. It has to burn itself out. The samskara, or conditioning, although capable of being burnt out, *cannot be seen.* You can never look at desire. Seeing desire will blind you. Your culture, your philosophy, your society has conditioned you, and now you think you can change or in some way modify that conditioning. It is impossible, for you are society.

We do not want to be free of conditioning. It is too frightening to contemplate. We are too insecure.

Every thought that is born has to die. It is what they call the death wish. If a thought does not die, it cannot be reborn. It has to die, and with it you die. But you don't die with each thought and breath. You hook up each thought with the next, creating a false continuity. It is *that* continuity that is the problem. Your insecurity springs from your refusal to face the temporary nature of thought. It is a little easier to talk to those who have attempted thought control—who have done some sadhana—because they experience the futility of it and can see where they are "hung up."

I suppose, then, that it is the tradition and conditioning that has created the moral dilemma for us?

Only the man who is capable of immorality can talk of morality. There is no such thing as immorality for me. I cannot sit and preach morality. That is all. I take no moral positions at all. The one who talks of morals, love, and compassion is a humbug.

Your morality or the lack of it is of no importance compared to the fact that *you are dead.* You are always operating in and through your dead memory. Memory is nothing more than the same old nonsense repeating itself, that's all. All you know, or can ever know, is memory, and memory is thought. Your ceaseless thinking is only giving you continuity. Why do you have to do that all the time? It is not worth it. You are wearing yourself out. When there is a need for it, one can understand. Why do you have to separate yourself from your actions and tell yourself all the time, "Now I am happy," "Now I feel I belong," "Now I feel alone"? Why? You are constantly monitoring and censoring your actions and feelings: "Now I feel this, now I feel that," "I want to be that," "I should not have done that." You are mulling over the future or the past all the time, oblivious to the present. There is no future in relation to your problem. Any solution you think of is in the future, and is, therefore, useless. If there is anything that can happen, it must happen *now*. Since you don't want anything to happen *now*, you push it away into something you have named "the future." What you have in place of the present is *fear*. Then begins the whole exhausting search for a way to be free from fear. Do you really want *this* kind of freedom? I say you do not.

Anything you want to be free from, for whatever reason, is the very thing that can free you. You have to be free from the very thing you want to be free from. You are always dealing with a pair of opposites, so being free of one is to be free from the other, its opposite. Within the framework of the opposites there is no freedom. That is why I always say, "You haven't got a chance..." Likewise, the man who is not concerned with morality will not be interested in immorality. The answer to selfishness lies in selfishness, not a fictitious opposite called selflessness. Freedom from anger lies in anger, not in non-anger. Freedom from greed lies in greed, not in non-greed.

The whole religious business is nothing but moral codes of conduct: you must be generous, compassionate, loving, while all the time you remain greedy and callous. Codes of conduct are set by society in its own interests, sacred or profane. There is nothing religious about it. The religious man puts the priest, the censor, inside you. Now the policeman has been institutionalized and placed outside you. Religious codes and strictures are no longer necessary; it is all in the civil and criminal codes.

You needn't bother with these religious people anymore, they are obsolete. But they don't want to lose their hold over people. It is their business, their livelihood is at stake. There is no difference between the policeman and the religious man. It is a little more difficult with the policeman, for, unlike the inner authority sponsored by the holy men, he lies outside you and must be bribed.

The helplessness of the average man to solve these basic dilemmas is acknowledged by many religions. Seekers are directed, therefore, to a sage, savior, or avatara. Yet you deny even this source of help and inspiration, do you not?

When you are suffering greatly and are very depressed, the body falls asleep. It is nature's way of handling the situation. Or you use repetitive words as a soporific—what you call *japa*—and go into sound sleep. You invent a name like Rama, repeat it endlessly, and hope to get some benefit. First of all you have invented Rama. Rama doesn't exist except as a historical figure. Having created the monster, you worship and then say you can't get out of it. It's alright with me if you continue with your *"Ram Nam."*

The repetition of holy names is a sincere effort to find something transcending the transient, something more permanent.

There is no permanence. The attempt to attain permanent happiness and uninterrupted pleasure is only choking the body, doing it violence. Your search for happiness only succeeds in destroying the sensitivity and intelligence of the nervous system. Wanting what does not exist—the romantic, religious, spiritual stuff—only adds momentum to that false continuity which destroys the body. It is radically disturbing the chemical balance of the body. The body, which is only interested in survival and procreation, treats both pain and pleasure alike. It is *you* who insist on stopping pain and extending pleasure. The body's response to both pleasure and pain is the same—it groans.

What does the body want? It doesn't want anything except to function. All other things are the inventions of thought. The body has no separate independent existence of its own apart from pleasure and pain. The various vibrations affecting the body may differ in intensity, but it is you who divide them into good and bad.

You are constantly translating vibrations that hit the body into experiences. You touch the table and it is "hard," you touch the pillow and it is "soft," you touch the woman's arm there and it is "sexy," and you touch the doorknob and it is "not-sexy." Without the constant translation of the sensory activity you have no way of knowing if something is hard, or soft, or sexy. The body's natural intelligence is correctly "processing" the sensory input without your having to do a thing. It is similar to how the body turns over many times during sleep without your being aware of it, much less trying to control it. The body is handling itself.

You are all the time interfering with the natural functioning of the nervous system. When a sensation hits your nervous system the first thing you do is to name it and categorize it as pleasure or pain. The next step is that you want to *continue* the pleasurable sensations and *stop* the painful sensations. First, the recognition of a sensation as pleasure or pain is itself painful. Second, the attempt to extend the life of one kind of sensation (pleasure), and to stop another kind of sensation (pain), is also painful. Both activities are choking the body. In the very nature of things every sensation has its own intensity and duration. The attempt to extend pleasure and stop pain only succeeds in destroying the sensitivity of the body and its ability to respond to sensations. So, what you are doing is very painful for the body.

If you *do nothing* with the sensations, you will find that they must dissolve into themselves. That is what I mean when I speak of the "ionization of thought." That is what I meant by birth and death. There is no "death" for the body, only disintegration. Thought being material, all its pursuits are material. That is why your so-called spiritual pursuits have no meaning. Don't get me wrong, I am not against using thought to get what you need; you have no other tool at your disposal.

So, the body is interested only in its survival. All that are necessary for life are the survival and reproductive systems. That is nature's way. *Why* life wants to reproduce itself is another matter. The only way the human organism can survive and ensure its reproduction is through thought. So thought is very important and even essential to the living organism. Thought determines whether there is action or no action. All animals have these survival thoughts, but, in the case of man, the factor of recognition is introduced, complicating the whole thing enormously. We have superimposed over the natural sensory functioning a never-ending verbalization.

The body is not at all interested in psychological or spiritual matters. Your highly praised spiritual experiences are of no value to the organism. In fact they are painful to the body. Love, compassion, *ahimsa,* understanding, bliss, all these things which religion and psychology have placed before man, are only adding to the strain of the body. *All* cultures, whether of the Orient or of the Occident, have created this lopsided situation for mankind and turned man into a neurotic individual. Instead of being what you are—unkind—you pursue the fictitious opposite put before you—kindness. To emphasize what we *should* be only causes strain, giving momentum to what we already in fact are. In nature we find the animals at one time violent and brutal, at others kind and generous. For them there is no contradiction. But man is told he must be always good, kind, loving, and never greedy or violent. We emphasize only one side of reality, thus distorting the whole picture. This trying to have one without the other is creating tremendous strain, sorrow, pain, and misery for man. Man must face the necessary violence in life; you must kill to live, one form of life thrives on another. And yet you have condemned killing.

If you don't mind, I would like to discuss another topic with you. What is the connection between deep sleep and death? In either case the "me" is absent, and yet they seem different.

Why are you talking of deep sleep? If there is any such thing as deep sleep, it's not possible for the sleeping person to know anything about it. So don't talk of deep sleep; it is something you can never know. The actual deep, natural, profound sleep natural to the body has nothing to do with poetic stuff like "dying to all your yesterdays." At the profoundest levels of rest, or deep sleep, the whole body goes through the death process, and may or may not return to vigor and normal waking states. If it comes around and is revived, it means that the body has not lost its ability to rejuvenate itself. What is left there after this death is free to carry on after its renewal. Actually, you are born and die with every breath you take. That is what is meant by death and rebirth.

Your thought structure denies the reality of death. It seeks continuity at all costs. I am not informing you about deep sleep or any other theories, but only pointing out that if you go deep enough the "you" disappears, the body goes through an actual clinical death, and that, in some cases, the body can renew itself. At that point the entire history of the individual, located in the body's genetic structure, no longer separates itself from life and falls into its own rhythm. From then on it cannot separate itself from anything.

What you experience in your ordinary superficial sleep is nature pushing down the thoughts so that the body and brain can rest. If the thoughts are not effectively pushed down into the subterranean regions, there will be no sleep. But after this deep sleep, there is no more sleep for the body. The entity that was there before informing itself, "Now I am asleep" and "Now I am awake" is no longer to be found. You can no longer create this division in consciousness between waking and sleeping. So don't bother theorizing about thoughtless states, when thought is finished, you die. Until then all talk of thoughtless states are the silly products of thought trying to give itself continuity by believing and searching out a thoughtless state. If you have ever fancied yourself to be in a thoughtless state, it means that thought was there.

The yogins maintain that it is possible to extend normal waking consciousness into the realms usually guarded by sleep, that is, into the unconscious.

You need not practice any yogic techniques in order to experience these things. By taking drugs you can have all these experiences. I am not at all advocating drugs any more than I am advocating yoga. I am just pointing out that all experience is born out of thought and is in all the essentials identical. If you call these yogic or drug-induced states blissful, more profound, or in any way more pleasurable than "ordinary" experiences, you are strengthening the ego and fortifying the separative structure by wasting your thoughts translating sensations into higher or lower and pleasurable or painful. Anything you experience as energy is thought-induced energy. It is not the energy of life.

What you are saying is contrary to what the religions and saints have…

The gurus can say what they want. The books can say all they like. It is advantageous to them. They are in the filthy market-place selling some shoddy goods.

But they say…

Forget them. What are *you,* essentially? What do *you* have to say? You have nothing to say. To sit and quote another is easy, but will do no good here.

Look. In this state there is no division. Our situation is that I cannot transmit and you cannot receive that fact. In addition to it, you have gone one step further and created a more complex problem for yourself by placing the undivided state outside yourself as you are; this means search. To search is to be cunning. The search for peace is dulling the natural peacefulness of the body. Your knowledge and search are meaningless because there is *nothing* inside the division you have created around you.

Because you disagree with some of the great teachings in some things, is that any reason to so ruthlessly brush aside the entire spiritual heritage of mankind?

It is all worthless as far as you are concerned. It is a menu without the meal. It is all a sales pitch. It has resulted in hypocrisy and commercialism. There is something radically wrong with it. If there is anything good, it cannot produce anything bad. Obviously, religions are false—religion, spirituality, society, you, your property, your motives and values, the whole thing.

It may be that the means have been corrupted, as you say. But the goal —bliss—seems to be a fundamental urge. Is this not so?

Bliss—what is that? Are you in a blissful state? You say that the atma is blissful, quoting your gurus and Mandukya Upanishad[6]. It is false, junk food. You don't have to indulge in all this nonsense to be free from it. You need not be a former drunkard in order to appreciate sobriety.

But it is so extraordinary to read the scriptures, they are inspirational.

What do these words mean to you? What do all these Sanskrit words mean to you? Don't start repeating what you have read. Do you have anything to say with regard to the way you are actually functioning right now? That is what is very important, not what Samkara[7] or someone else has said. I am not here to teach you anything. This is not a didactic or instructional exercise. The fact that you have chosen to come here and ask these questions means that all those gurus and scriptures have failed you, does it not? If you do not come here, you will go somewhere else. Words only have a vague abstract meaning for you; otherwise, they have no relevance to you at all.

All this has been a bit disillusioning. May I go and continue this conversation tomorrow?

Of course.

Thank you.

• • • •

Where is space? Is there space without the four walls? What tells you that there is something called space? Don't repeat what others have said on this question. Without thought is there space at all? There is not. Thought creates time as well as space. The moment thought is there, there is time and space.

Thought has created tomorrow. You feel hopeless because you have created tomorrow's hope. Your only chance is now—no hope is necessary. Neither is the idea of self or atma valid. I tried so hard to find one. It was wrongly put together by the philosophers.

Thought is body, thought is life, thought is sex. You are the thought. Thought is you. If there is no thought, you are not there. There is no world, if thought is not there.

My God, what a mess! How can I save myself from all this? It is a sad destiny to contemplate.

You have to be saved from the very idea that you have to be saved. You must be saved from the saviors, redeemed from the redeemers. If it is to happen, it must happen *now*. My words cannot penetrate the lunacy there. It is the madness of the spiritual search that makes you unmoved and impervious to my words. The line between the madman and the mystic is a very, very thin one. The madman is regarded as a clinical case, while the other, the mystic, is equally pathological.

Forget the rosaries, the scriptures, the ashes on your forehead. When you see for yourself the absurdity of your search, the whole culture is reduced to ashes inside you. Then you are out of that. Tradition is finished for you. No more games. *Vedanta* means the end of knowledge. So why write more holy books, open more schools, preserve more teachings? The burning up inside you of everything you want is the meaning of ashes. When you know nothing, you say a lot. When you know something, there is nothing to say.

The state of not knowing you describe is related to another level of consciousness. What has it got to do with me, an ordinary neurotic person?

What levels of consciousness? There are no levels of consciousness. Awareness is no different in the waking state than in the sleeping state. Even while you are sitting here you are dreaming. There cannot be dreaming without images. When you are lying in bed you call it dreaming, when sitting with the eyes open you call it something else, that is all. For me these images are absent, whether I am in a "waking" or a "sleeping" state. I cannot form any image at any time. It does not matter here whether the eyes are open or closed. The only thing that is there in that individualized consciousness is the sure reflection of what is presented to it. You do not name it. The movement or desire to know what it is simply is not there. I have no way of knowing or experiencing this so-called wakeful state. I can mechanically explain the wakeful state, but this does *not* imply that there is someone there who *knows that he is awake.* The explanations don't mean a thing. That is why I maintain that your natural state is one of "not knowing."

Most schools of religion and psychology recommend the expansion or intensification of awareness as a means to a more fulfilled life, as, for example, through therapy. Is this what you are talking about—some kind of awareness therapy?

No. Awareness is a simple activity of the brain. It cannot be used to bring about *any* change, including a therapeutic one. We have superimposed a naming process over this natural physiological awareness, an awareness we share, incidentally, with the other animals. Awareness and the movement or tendency in you to bring about change in you are two different things entirely. That difference cannot be perceived by you, for there is no perception without the perceiver. Can you become conscious of anything except through the medium of memory and thought? Memory is knowledge. Even your feelings are memory. The stimulus and the response form one unitary movement—they cannot be neatly separated.

In other words, you cannot even differentiate the stimulus from the response; there is no dividing line, except when thought steps in and creates one. Thought, as memory and knowledge, has created this mechanism. The only way it can perpetuate itself is to gather knowledge, to know more and more, to ask more and more questions. As long as you are seeking you will be asking questions, and the questioning mechanism only adds more momentum to the naming process.

But let us not sell thought short. It can capture many wonderful things.

Thought can never capture the movement of life, it is much too slow. It is like lightning and thunder. They occur simultaneously, but sound, traveling slower than light, reaches you later, creating the illusion of two separate events. It is only the natural physiological sensations and perceptions that can move with the flow of life. There is no question of capturing or containing that movement. We like to use the word consciousness glibly, as if we are intimately familiar with it. Actually, consciousness is something we will never know.

So attempts to suspend thought, somehow hoping to be purely aware, is bogus?

As far as I am concerned we become conscious of something only through memory, knowledge. Otherwise space, and the separative consciousness it creates, are not there. There is no such thing as looking at something without the interference of knowledge. To look you need space, and thought creates that space. So space itself, as a dimension, exists only as a creation of thought. Thought has also tried to theorize about the space it has created, inventing the "time-space-continuum." Time is an independent reference or frame. There is no necessary continuity between it and space.

Thought has also invented the opposite of time, the "now," the "eternal now." The present exists only as an idea. The moment you attempt to look at the present, it has already been brought into the framework of the past.

Thought will use any trick under the sun to give momentum to its own continuity. Its essential technique is to repeat the same thing over and over again; this gives it an illusion of permanency. This permanency is shattered the moment the falseness of the past-present-future continuum is seen. The future can be nothing but the modified continuity of the past.

These philosophical endeavors only seem to complicate things. Is it not possible to live simply with nature, to look at the clouds and trees?

The tree you are talking about cannot be captured by thought. If your thought structure cannot stop and frame its reflection of the tree, you have no way of looking at the tree at all. In other words, the tree is actually looking at you, not vice versa. I am not trying to mystify it. The important thing to see is the false separation between you and the tree, not who is looking at whom. Approaching the reality of the "positively" or "negatively," as the philosophers try to do, has no meaning. The gap, created by thought, remains, no matter what approach you take.

Thought has created all these divisions, making what you call experience possible. The man who has freed himself from all divisions in consciousness has no experiences; he does not have "loving" relationships, does not question anything, has no notions about being a self-realized man, and is not stuck on wanting to help somebody else.

What I am maintaining is that the whole problem has been created by culture. It is that that has created this neurotic division in man. Somewhere along the line man separated himself and experienced self-consciousness—which the other animals don't have—for the first time. This has created misery for man. That is the beginning of the end of man.

The individual who is able, through luck, to be free from this self-consciousness, is no longer experiencing an independent existence. He is, even to himself, like any other thing out there. What happens in the environment repeats itself within such an individual, without the knowledge. Once thought has burnt itself out, nothing that creates division can remain there.

While thought is taking birth, the disintegration or death of thought is taking place also. That is why it is not natural for thought to take root. Only by maintaining a divisive consciousness in man is thought capable of denying the harmonious functioning of the body. To cast man in religious or psychological terms is to deny the extraordinary intelligence of this wondrous body. It is the movement of thought that is constantly taking you away from your natural state and creating this division.

Is there any way for us to experience, much less share, reality? Forget about ultimate reality; you have no way of experiencing the reality of anything. Experiencing reality from moment to moment is also a thought-induced state of mind.

Listening to you is difficult for us, for what you are saying undermines the very basis of communication.

You cannot listen to anybody without interpretation. There is no such thing as "the art of pure listening." You can sit here talking for the rest of your life without getting anywhere. Without a common reference point—which is another invention of thought—how can you communicate and share? It is just not possible. There is nothing *to* communicate anyhow.

You want to use communication to help you out of the mess you are in. That is your only interest. Getting out of your situation is your only aim. Why? Why do you want to get out of your situation? Wanting to get out of situations is what has created the problem in the first place. Wanting to free yourself from the burden is really the problem. I am not recommending anything; doing or not doing lead to the same end: misery. So doing nothing is no different from doing something. As long as you have knowledge about that burden—which I deny exists— you will have to struggle to be free of it. It cannot but do otherwise. Anything you do is part of the mechanism of thought.

Your search for happiness is prolonging your unhappiness.

There is a ring of certainty and authority in what you say. We want to know…

From whom do you want to know? Not from me. I don't know. If you assume that I know, you are sadly mistaken. I have no way of knowing. What is there inside you is only the movement of knowledge wanting to know more and more. The "you," the separative structure can continue only as long as there is a demand to know. That is the reason why you are asking these questions, not to find out anything for yourself. Nothing you can tell yourself can change your unfortunate situation. Why should something, or nothing, happen?

The demand for freedom, whether outwardly or inwardly, has been with us for a long while. We have been told that this demand is a sacred, noble thing. Have we again been misled?

The demand to be free is the cause of your problems. You want to see yourself as free. The one that is saying, "You are not free," is the same one that is telling you that there is a state of "freedom" to be pursued. But the pursuit is slavery, the very denial of freedom. I do not know anything about freedom, because I do not know anything about myself, free, enslaved, or otherwise. Freedom and self-knowledge are linked. Since I do not know myself and have no way of seeing myself, except by the knowledge given me by my culture, the question of wanting to be free does not arise at all. The knowledge you have about freedom denies the very possibility of freedom. When you stop looking at yourself with the knowledge you have, the demand to be free from that self drops away.

Our ordinary minds are too cluttered to appreciate what you are saying. Only a profoundly still mind can begin to understand you. Is this not so?

Stillness of mind is ridiculous. There is no such thing as stillness of mind. This is another trick created by the demand to be free. What is there is the constant demand to be free. Nothing else is there. How can you, and why should you, be free from memory? Memory is absolutely essential. The problem is not having a memory, but your tendency to use memory to further your "spiritual" interests, or as a means to find happiness. To attempt to be free from memory is withdrawal, and withdrawal is death.

There is nothing to know. The statement that there is nothing to know is an abstraction to you, because you know. To you not knowing is a myth. What is there is not not-knowing but knowing projecting the state of freeing yourself from the known. Your demand to be free from the known is the one that is creating the problem. As long as the notion of "I ought to be this" is there, then so long will that which I actually am be there.

So it is the fantasizing about a non-existent ideal person, society, or state that dooms and fixes me where I am. My belief in what I am not determines what I in fact am. Is that it?

That's it. And the greatest ideal, the most imposing, perfect and powerful, is, of course, God. It is an invention of frightened minds. The human mind has many destructive inventions to its credit. The most destructive one, and the one that has corrupted you, is the invention of God. The history of human thinking has produced saints, teachers, gurus, bhagavans, but God is the most corrupt of them all. Man has already messed up his life, and religion has made it worse. It is religion that really made a mess of man's life.

One parallel I have noticed between your message and other teachings, especially that of J. Krishnamurti, is the stress on the thought structure and its ability to blind us. Why is thought so important?

It is important that although thought controls and determines your every action, it, at the same time, cannot itself be seen by consciousness. You can think and theorize *about* thought but cannot perceive or appreciate thought itself. Are you and thought two separate things? You know *about* thought, not thought itself. Does thought exist apart from the knowledge you have *about* thought? About all you can say is, "I know, I have knowledge about my thoughts, about my experiences, about this or that," that is all you can do. Independent of that, is there thought? Your knowing about thought is the only thing there is.

So all that is there is the knowledge you have accumulated about thought. Nothing else is there. All the things observed, as well as the observer himself, are part of this knowledge about thought. They are thoughts, and the "I" is another thought. But there is no individual value in thought; it is not yours, it belongs to everyone, like the atmosphere. Knowledge is common property.

What I am trying to say is that there is no individual there at all. There is only a certain gathering of knowledge—which is thought—but no individuality there. The knowledge you have of things is all that you are capable of experiencing. Without knowledge no experience of any kind is possible. You cannot separate experience and knowledge. The "I" is nothing sacred; it is the totality of your knowledge, and you are, unfortunately, stuck with it. Why are you interested in separating the knowledge you have about yourself—whatever you call yourself? Knowledge is all that is there. Where is the "I"? You have separated the "I" from the knowledge it has of the things about you. It is an illusion.

Similarly, enlightenment has no independent existence of its own apart from your knowledge about it. There is no enlightenment at all. The idea of illumination is tied up with change, but there is nothing *to* change. Change admits of time; change *always* takes time. To change, to eliminate one thing and replace it with another, takes time. What you are now and what you ought to be are linked together by time. You are going to be enlightened *tomorrow*.

Let us take this as an example. You want to be enlightened, you want to be "selfless"; you are this, you want to be that. The gap between the two is filled with time, put there to ask the repetitive question, "How?" Your enlightenment or selflessness is always tomorrow, not now. So time is essential, and time is thought. Thinking is not action, not taking, but merely wanting. You are not ready to do a thing, only meditate, which is just thinking about it. Your thought structure, which is *you,* can't conceive of the possibility of anything happening except in time. This escapist logic is also applied by everyone to spiritual matters, only the time frame is larger. It happens in a future life or perhaps in heaven; at any rate, tomorrow. And just as there is no tomorrow in these matters, so its reference point, the present, does not exist. Where does it not exist? In thought, which is the past. There is no question of enlightenment and selfless "now," because there is no "now," only the projection of the present into the past.

You have never seen a tree, only your knowledge you have about trees. You see the knowledge, not the tree. Your whole interest in selflessness is motivated by the past. As long as there is motivation, it is a self-centered activity. The more you do, the more selfish you become. Your wanting to be enlightened or selfless is a very selfish thing. You don't want freedom, nor do you want everyone to be free, you want "freedom" for *you.* With an approach like that, how the hell are you going to be free? You are not going to be free.

There Is Nothing *to* *Understand*

You will never be free from selfishness.

But all the saints, saviors and religions of all times have encouraged us to be unselfish, to be self-effacing, to be meek. It must therefore be possible. How can you be so certain of such a thing?

Because it is crystal clear to me that you have invented this idea of selflessness to protect yourself from the actual—your selfishness. In any case, whether you believe in selflessness or not, you remain at all times selfish. Your so-called selflessness exists only in the future, tomorrow. And when tomorrow comes, it is put off until the next day, or perhaps next life.

Look at it this way; it is like the horizon. Actually, there is no horizon. The more you move towards the horizon, the more it moves away. It is only the limitations of the eyes that creates the horizon. But there is no such thing as the horizon. Likewise, there is no such thing as selflessness at all. Man has tortured himself for generations with this idea of selflessness, and it has only afforded a living for those who sell the idea of selflessness for a living, like the priests and moralists.

I am not condemning you or anyone else, just pointing out the absurdity of what you are doing.

When the energy that is spent in the pursuit of something that does not exist, like selflessness, is released, your problem becomes very simple, no matter what it is. You will cease to create problems on the material plane, and that's the only plane there is.

Yes, but what about those who are not searching for some illusory abstraction, but simply happiness?

Their search for happiness is no different from the spiritual pursuit. It is the pursuit of pleasure, spirituality being the greatest, ultimate pleasure.

So this pursuit has to go?

Don't say it should go. Wanting selfishness to go is part and parcel of the selfish pursuit of a more pleasurable state—selflessness. Both do not exist. That is why you are eternally unhappy. Your search for happiness is making you unhappy. Both the spiritual goal and the search for happiness are the same. Both are essentially selfish, pleasurable pursuits. If that understanding is somehow there in you, then you will not use the energy in that direction at all.

You know, I've been everywhere in the world, and have found that people are exactly the same. There is no difference at all. *Becoming* is the most important thing in the world for everybody—to become something. They all want to become rich, whether materially or spiritually, it is exactly the same. Don't divide it—the so-called spiritual is the materialistic. You may think you are superior because you go to temple and do *puja*, but the woman there is doing puja in the hope of having a child.

She wants something, so she goes to the temple. So do you; it is exactly the same. For sentimental reasons you go, but in time it will become routine and become abhorrent to you.

What I am trying to point out is simply this: your spiritual and religious activities are basically selfish. That is all I am pointing out. You go to the temple for the same reason you go other places—you want some result. If you don't want anything there is no reason to go to the temple.

But the great majority of people go to the temple.

Why are you so concerned about what the majority does? This is your problem, and you must solve it for yourself. Don't bother about mankind and all the billions of people in the world.

You are ruthlessly condemning whatever people have said so far. You may, in time, also be condemned and blasted for what you are saying.

If you have the guts, I will be the very first to salute you. But you must not rely on your holy books—the Bhagavad Gita[8] or Upanishads. You must challenge what I am saying without the help of your so-called authorities. You just don't have the guts to do that because you are relying upon the Gita, not upon yourself. That is why you will never be able to do it. If you have that courage, you are the only person who can falsify what I am saying. A great sage like Gowdapada[9] can do it, but he is not here. You are merely repeating what Gowdapada[i] and others have said. It is a worthless statement as far as you are concerned. If there were a living Gowdapada sitting here, he would be able to blast what I am saying, but not you. So don't escape into meaningless generalizations. You must have the guts to disprove what I am saying on your own. What I am saying must be false for you. You can only agree or disagree with what I am saying according to what some joker has told you. That is not the way to go about it.

I am just pointing out that there are no solutions at all, only problems. If others have said the same thing I am saying, why are you asking questions and searching for solutions here? Forget about the masses; I am talking about you. You are merely looking for new, better methods. I am not going to help you. I am saying, "Don't bother about solutions; try to find out what the problem is." The problem is the solution; solutions just don't solve your problem. Why in the hell are you looking for another solution? Don't come to me for solutions. That is all I am saying. You will make out of what I am saying another solution, to be added to your list of solutions, which are all useless when it comes to actually solving your problems.

What I am saying is valid and true for me, that is all. If I suggest *anything,* directly or indirectly, you will turn it into another method or technique. I would be falsifying myself if I were to make any such suggestion.

If *anyone* says there is a way out, he is not an honest fellow. He is doing it for his own self-aggrandizement, you may be sure. He simply wants to market a product and hopes to convince you that it is superior to other products on the market. If another man comes along and says that there is no way out, you make of that another method. It is all a fruitless attempt to overtake your own shadow. And yet you can't remain where you are. *That* is the problem.

From all this you inevitably draw the conclusion that the situation is hopeless. In reality you are creating that hopelessness because you don't really want to be free from fear, envy, jealousy, and selfishness. That is why you feel your situation to be hopeless. The only hope lies in selfishness, greed, and anger, not in its fictitious opposite, i.e., the practice of selflessness, generosity, and kindness. The problem, say selfishness, is only strengthened by the cultivation of its fictitious opposite, the so-called selflessness.

Sitting here discussing these things is meaningless, useless. That is why I am always saying to my listeners, "Get lost, please!" What you want you can get elsewhere, but not here. Go to the temple, do puja, repeat mantras, put on ashes. Eventually some joker comes along and says, "Give me a week's wages and I will give you a better mantra to repeat." Then another fellow comes along and tells you not to do any of that, that it is useless, and that what he is saying is much more revolutionary. He prescribes "choiceless awareness," takes your money and builds schools, organizations, and tantric centers.

Why shouldn't we brush aside what you are saying, just as you brush aside the teachings and efforts of others?

You will never blast me; the attachment you have to religious authority prohibits you from questioning *anything,* much less a man like me. I am certain you will never challenge me. For that reason what I am saying will inevitably create an unstable, neurotic situation for you. You cannot accept what I am saying, and neither are you in any position to reject it. If it wasn't for your very thick skin, you would certainly end up in the loony bin. You simply cannot and will not question what I am saying; it is too much of a threat. Absolutely *nothing* is going to penetrate your defenses—Gowdapada provides the gloves, the Bhagavad Gita a snug coat jacket, and the Brahmasutra[10] a bullet-proof vest. So you are safe, and that is all you are really interested in. You can't blast what I am saying as long as you are relying upon what someone has said before.

Please don't say that there are thousands of seers and sages; there are only a very few. You can count them all on your fingers. The rest are merely technocrats. The saint is a technocrat. That is what most people are. But now with the development of drugs and other techniques, the saint is dispensable. You don't any longer need a priest or saint to instruct you in meditation. If you want to control your thoughts, simply take a drug and forget them, if that is what you want. If you can't sleep, take a sleeping pill. Sleep for a while, then wake up. It is the same.

Don't listen to me. It will create an unnecessary disturbance in you. It will only intensify the neurotic situation you are already caught in. Having taken for granted the validity of all this holy stuff, having never questioned, much less broken away from it, you not only have learned how to live with it, but also how to capitalize on it. It is a matter of profiteering, nothing more.

If all this is so, then why do you go on talking?

There is no use asking me why I talk. Am I selling or promising you anything? I am not offering you peace of mind, am I? You counter by saying that I am taking away your precious peace of mind. On the contrary, I am singing my own song, just going my own way, and you come along and attempt to disturb my peace.

I feel that if anybody can help us it is you.

No sir! Anything I do to help would only add to your misery— that is all. By continuing to listen to me you merely heap one more misery upon those you already have. In that sense this discussion we are having is doing you no good whatever. You don't seem to realize that you are playing with fire here. If you really want moksha here and now, you can have it. You see, you *are* anger, selfishness, and all these things; if they go, you go. There is a physical going—not in the abstract, but actual physical death.

You are saying that that can happen now? Others have said...

I don't give a hoot what others have said. It can happen now. You simply don't want it. You would not touch it with a ten-foot barge pole. If anger and selfishness, which is *you,* go, moksha is now, not tomorrow. Your own anger will burn you, not the electric heater. So the religious man has invented selflessness. If that selflessness goes, you go, that is all. So, freeing yourself from any one of these things (i.e., greed, selfishness, etc.,) implies that you, as you know and experience yourself, are coming to an end *now*. Please, in your interest and out of compassion I am telling you, this is not what you want. This is not a thing you can make happen. It is not in your hands at all. It hits whomsoever it chooses. You are out of the picture altogether.

All that poetry and romanticism about "dying to all your yesterdays" is not going to help you, or anybody. Nothing can come out of it. They may hold forth on platforms, but they themselves don't want it. It is just words. Eventually people settle for that (i.e., temples, mantras, scriptures). It is all too absurd and childish.

Then how can we find out for ourselves and not just repeat the words of the so-called experts?

You have to actually touch life at a point where nobody has touched it before. Nobody can teach you that. As long as you continue to repeat what others have said before, you are lost, and nothing good can come of it. Listening to and believing what others have said is not the way to find out for yourself, and there is no other way.

So you are saying that we must get rid of our belief that...

Don't bother. You will replace one belief with another. You are nothing but belief, and when it dies, you are dead. What I am trying to tell you is this: don't try to be free from selfishness, greed, anger, envy, desire, and fear. You will only create its opposites, which are, unfortunately, fictitious. If desire dies, you die. The black van comes and carts you away, that's it! Even if you should somehow miraculously survive such a shock, it will be of *no use* to you, or to others.

You prefer to toy with things, asking absurd questions like, "What happens to my body after death? Will the body be strong enough to take it?" What the hell are you talking about? You are asking me what will happen to you if you touch that live electrical wire there. That is the kind of pointless question you are asking. You are not really interested at all. Perhaps after touching this you will be completely burnt and have to be thrown away. Perhaps others will get a shock themselves upon touching you, and you will become an untouchable!

Look at what is implied by what I am saying. If you have the courage to touch life for the first time, you will never know what hit you. Everything man has taught, felt, and experienced is gone, and nothing is put in its place. Such a person becomes the living authority by virtue of his freedom from the past and culture, and he will remain so until someone else who has discovered this for himself blasts it. Until you have the courage to blast me, all that I am saying, and all the gurus, you will remain a cultist with photographs, rituals, birthday celebrations, and the like.

I am sorry. I sing my song and go.

But we are lost, and so we need gurus, sadhana, and scriptures or guidance.

You can go back to your gurus. Do what you like. The thing I am talking about happens to the lucky; if you are lucky, you are lucky. That is all. I have nothing to do with it. It is in no one's hands.

Lucky or unlucky, our tradition tells us that life is transient, that all is in flux, that...

That is the tradition of India I am talking about—*change,* not the tradition you talk about, which is *no change.* Your whole life is a denial of the reality of change. You only wish to continue, somehow, then revive, only to continue. That is not the great tradition of India I am talking of. You think you are asking a profound question when you ask, "What is death?" You presume to ask Gowdapada's question before you have asked the more fundamental question, "Am I born?" Instead of tackling this basic question on your own, you quote and write commentaries upon Gowdapada, then take the easy way out, and simply equate what I am saying with what he said. That is your cop out.

In any event, all you can do is to speculate about death and reincarnation. Only dead people ask about death. Those who are really living would never ask such a question. That memory in you—which is dead—wants to know if it will continue even after what it imagines to be death. That is why it is asking such silly questions. Death is finality; you are dead only once. When once the questions and ideas you have have died, then you will never ask about death again.

You are ripping everything away, and suddenly I see that I have to strike out on my own, that no one can help me.

Are you sure that no one can help you? You are not so sure. So your statement doesn't mean anything. You will harbor hope. Even assuming for a moment that an outside force can help you, you are still convinced that *you can help yourself.* This gives you tremendous hope, and hope is *always* oriented towards achieving something. So, rather than waste your time asking if there is or is not anyone who can help you achieve what you want, you should rather be asking, "Is there anything to be attained?" Whether you yourself, or someone else, helps you to attain it is not the issue at all. It is, rather, that you are searching. That is obvious. But for what are you searching? You are undoubtedly searching for what you already know. It is impossible to search for something you do not know. You search for, and find, what you know. It is difficult for you to face this simple fact.

Please don't get me wrong. I am not asking questions, playing some kind of Socratic guessing game. I am not here to offer you any new methods, new techniques, or suggest any gimmicks to attain your goal. If other systems, techniques, and gimmicks have failed to help you reach your goal, and if you are looking or shopping around for some newer, better methods here, I am afraid I cannot be of any help to you. If you feel that someone else can help you, good luck to you. But I am compelled, through the lessons of my own experience, to add the rider, "You will get nowhere, you will see."

The uselessness of turning to inner or outer sources to help you is something of which I am certain. It is clear to me that to find out for yourself you must be absolutely helpless with nowhere to turn. That is all. Unfortunately, this certainty cannot be transmitted to someone else. The certainty I have is simply that the goal, which you have invented, is responsible for your search. As long as the goal is there, so long will the search for it continue. If you say, "I really don't know what I am searching for," that is not true. So, what is it that you are searching for? That is by far the most important question to ask yourself.

If you look at it you will see that, aside from your natural physical needs, what you want has arisen from what you have been told, what you have read, and what you yourself have experienced. The physical wants are self-evident and easily understandable. But this particular want—the object of your search—is something born out of your thinking, which in turn is based upon the knowledge you have gathered from various sources.

If all you say is true, we are in a bad way indeed. We are not in a position to accept or reject what you are saying. Why, then, do you go on talking to us? What meaning can it have?

This dialogue with you has no meaning at all. You may very well ask why the hell I am talking. I emphatically assure you that, in my case, it is not at all in the nature of self-fulfillment. My motive for talking is quite different from what you think it is. It is not that I am eager to help you understand, or that I feel that I must help you. Not at all. My motive is direct and temporary: you arrive seeking understanding, while I am only interested in making it crystal clear that *there is nothing to understand.*

As long as you want to understand, so long there will be this awkward relationship between two individuals. I am always emphasizing that somehow the truth has to dawn upon you that there is nothing to understand. As long as you think, accept, and believe that there is something to understand, and make that understanding a goal to be placed before you, demanding search and struggle, you are lost and will live in misery.

I have only a few things to say and I go on repeating them again and again and again. There are no questions for me, other than the practical questions for everyday functioning in this world. You, however, have many, many questions. These questions all have the same source: your knowledge. It is simply not in the nature of things that you can have a question without knowing the answer already. So meaningful dialogue is simply not possible when you are asking questions to yourself and to me, because you have already made up your mind, you already possess the answers. So communication between us is impossible; what is the point of carrying on any dialogue?

There is the actual need to be free from answers themselves. The search is invalid because it is based upon questions which in turn are based upon false knowledge. Your knowledge has not freed you from your problems. Your dilemma is that you are searching for answers to questions you already know the answer to. This is making you neurotic. If the questions you have were actually solvable, it, the question, would blow itself up. Because all questions are merely variations on the same question, the annihilation of one means the annihilation of all. So freedom exists not in finding answers, but in the dissolution of all questions. This sort of problem-solving you are not, unfortunately, the least interested in.

What others and you yourself think are the answers cannot help you at all. It is really very simple—if the answer is correct, the question disappears. I have no questions of any kind. They never enter my head. All my questions, which resolved themselves into one great question, have disappeared entirely. The questioner simply realized that it was meaningless to go on asking questions, the answers to which I already knew. You have foolishly created this search as an answer to your questions, which in turn have been invented out of the knowledge you have gathered. The questions you are formulating are born out of answers you already have. So what is your goal? You must be very clear about it, otherwise there is no point in proceeding. It becomes a game, a meaningless ritual.

What do you want to get? There is always somebody to help you get what you want, for a price. You have foolishly divided life into higher and lower goals, into material and spiritual paths. In either case great struggle, pain, and effort is involved. I say, on the other hand, that there are no spiritual goals at all; they are simply the extension of material goals into what you imagine to be a higher, loftier plane. You mistakenly believe that by pursuing the spiritual goal you will somehow miraculously make your material goals simple and manageable. Such pursuits are in actuality not possible. You may think that only inferior persons pursue material goals, that material achievements are boring. But in fact the so-called spiritual goals you have put before yourself are exactly the same. You are your search, and it will not help to think that you have understood and are free of this. If you don't come here, you will go elsewhere in search of answers.

Discovering the reality you are talking about demands real relationship and open communication with others, does it not?

Forget it, sir! Dialogue has no meaning. Neither has conversation any meaning. What the hell are we doing? Do you think that I talk with people as an excuse of some kind? Do you think that I harbor any illusions about communicating with you? I have no such illusions. The very fact that you have returned here again to talk and discuss shows that you have not heard a thing I am saying. Once that understanding is there, the whole thing is finished for you once and for all. You will not visit any gurus, read any books on this, or listen to anybody. You will not stupidly repeat what others have said, especially what the holy men, saints, and saviors have said. All that is washed out of the system and you are left incapable of following or listening to anyone, not even a God walking the face of the earth, or even a million gods rolled into one. What good is it, after all, when somebody has a billion dollars and you are wondering where your next meal will come from? Anyway, that's not the point. The important thing is: what do you *want*? Please let us forget about your bhagavans. Don't sit here and repeat what you have heard from your gurus, it is useless. When once you place your hope, belief, and confidence in your guru, you are stuck with him.

Virtually all the gurus, at least the Eastern ones, have stressed the necessity of being free from one's conditioning, one's past.

The past will always be there as long as you want something. Even if you attempt to suppress your wants, the past has to come to your help and tell you *how* to suppress your wants. There is no such differentiation of wants; they are all exactly the same. In the Indian culture the spiritual wants are extolled and sought after, while in the West the material wants prevail.

When wanting ceases, even for a moment, thought is absent and you are left with the simple matter of taking care of the bodily wants—food, clothes, and shelter. To practice some sort of twisted self-denial in which you fail to see to the body's actual physical needs is a silly, perverted way of living.

But the key question remains: how is one not to want?

Again you ask "how," thus avoiding the issue. There is no "how" at all. "How" is the trickiest question, for in asking it you are doomed. "How to live?" That is one question that has been bothering people for centuries. Religions claim to give a satisfactory answer to this question. Every teacher claims he knows how. He will be pleased to show you how, for a fee of course. "How to live one's life?" That is the one question which has transformed itself into millions of questions. That is all.

Brushing aside the question of how to be free from constant wanting, it seems obvious from what you have said that one must be free first from the influence of the past, or one's memory. Is this not so?

If you go on trying to suppress the past, trying to live in what you call "the present," you will drive yourself crazy. You are trying to control something over which you have no control. It is just not possible to control thought without becoming neurotic, for it is not just your personal, petty little past that is in the way, but the entire past of mankind, the entire memory of every human being, every form of life, and every form of existence. It is not such a simple, easy thing to do. If you try to control the natural flow of the river through all these artificial means—building a dam so to speak—you will inundate and destroy the whole thing. That is why you find thoughts welling up inside you despite your efforts to control, observe, and be aware of them. Once this is understood, then you are never concerned whether thoughts are there or not. When there is an actual need for thought to function, it is there; when there is no need for thought to function, it is not there. You don't even know, and have no way of finding out, whether you are thinking or not. Your *constant* utilization of thought to give continuity to your separative self *is you*. There is nothing there inside you other than that. What you call the "you" is nothing other than the continuity of thought. If that artificial continuity is not there, neither are you. The "you" wants only to function on a different, "higher" level, and not to come to an end. You want to be transformed, to become something else, while continuing. The only way the self can do that is to add more and more experiences to those it has already accumulated.

How does this process of accumulation work?

The *only* way the self can add more and more knowledge and experience is to endlessly ask itself the meaningless question "How? How am I to live?" If someone tells you that the continuity of knowledge and experience must come to an end, you ask, "How?", and are right back in the same trap. You are merely asking for the same kind of knowledge.

But we just want to know about enlightenment, if it is possible.

You want to know whether there is enlightenment or not, who has it, and how to get it. You are curious about how a supposedly enlightened man would behave, what is the nature of his behavior patterns, and so on. Apparently you know a great deal about enlightenment; you must, for you are searching for it.

Not all of us are so naive as to think we can directly search for God, enlightenment, or nirvana. *So we can accept the illusory nature of such goals. But we are searching for more practical, tangible things like…*

People are looking for enlightenment. You say you are not, but it is the same. Whether you want a new car or simple peace of mind, it is still a painful search. The secular leaders tell you one way, the holy men another way. It makes no difference—as long as you are searching for peace of mind, you will have a tormented mind. If you try not to search, or if you continue to search, you will remain the same. You have to *stop*. You don't stop searching because such an act would be the end of you.

You are lost in a jungle, and you have no way of finding your way out. Night is fast approaching, the wild animals are there, including the cobras, and still you are lost. What do you do in such a situation? You just stop. You don't move.

But we can never be absolutely sure that there is not some way out, no matter how fantastic or improbable it may be.

As long as there is that hope that you can somehow or the other get out of the jungle, so long will you continue what you are doing—searching—and so long you feel lost. You are lost only because you are searching. You have no way of finding your way out of the jungle.

So if one could just stop…

No, that's not it at all. You still expect something to happen. That expectation is part of the problem. That is why you are pursuing these questions. Your expectations are part of your desire to change everything. Nothing needs changing; you must accept life as it is. Through "change" you hope and expect to be born again. What the hell for? This life is enough. There is no peace in this life, no lack of unhappiness, so you wait until your next life to be happy. It's not worth it. You may very well *not* be born again. After all, it is only a hopeful theory to you. You may as well find out for yourself if it is possible to be at peace with yourself *now*.

But all our aspirations, whether material or spiritual, seem to be defined and cast in the mold of our societies, which are, like each of us, corrupt. Yet I must live and struggle within the limits my society has erected around me. My life is not determined solely by my personal aims and attributes, but by what my society allows me to do, that is, by what actual opportunities are made available.

You want so many things, and I am not in a position to help you get any of them. You are not clear what you really want. When that which you want is fully recognized, then you must find out how to get what you want. And either you get it or you don't, that's all. So don't bother separating your goals into the low and the lofty. You have been doing that all your life and have not succeeded.

Not just I, but everyone I know seems caught in this trap of endless searching and struggle. We need, do we not, to sit down together and communicate with each other on this?

As I said, I have no illusions about communication. You cannot share or communicate your experiences with anybody, because, the way you are now functioning, each individual lives in separate and different worlds without any common reference point, and only imagines that they ever communicate with another. It is just not possible.

I cannot communicate and you cannot understand because you have no reference point in regard to what I am saying. When once you have understood that there is nothing to understand, what is there to communicate? Communication is just not necessary. So there is no point in discussing the possibility of communication. Your desire to communicate is part of your general strategy of achievement. Veiled behind that desire for communication is the dependency upon some outside power to solve your problems for you. Except for the quite natural need for practical communication necessary to function in this world, your interest in communication is really an expression of your feelings of helplessness and your hope for the support of some outside agency. Your helplessness persists because of your dependency upon some outside agency. When that dependency upon some outside agency, fictitious or not, is not there, then the feelings of helplessness and the desire to communicate in the abstract, are not there. If the one goes, the other must go also. Your situation and prospects only seem hopeless because you have ideas of hope. Knock off that hope and the crippling feelings of helplessness go with it. There is bound to be helplessness and overwhelming frustration as long as you exist in relationship with the hope for fulfillment, because there is no fulfillment at all. This is the source of your dilemma.

All this is just too much to comprehend and act upon immediately. Perhaps at some time in the future, when I am more able...

The future is created by hope, that is the only future that exists. The hope of achieving your goal, the hope of attaining enlightenment, the hope of somehow getting off the merry-go-round—that is the future. The point from which you project yourself into the future appears to you to be the present, the now. But this is mistaken. There is only the past in operation, and that movement creates the illusion of present and future. You may find what I am saying here logical, or illogical, and you may accept or reject it. But it will in any case be the past that is doing so, for that is all that is in operation within you. It is the past that has projected these goals—God, enlightenment, peace of mind, whatever—and has placed them in the future, out of reach. So happiness is always in the future, tomorrow. A happy man wouldn't be interested in seeking happiness. A well-fed man is not in search of food.

Surely real understanding, of which we are all more or less capable, takes place not in the future, but now, in the present.

There is only the past. You have been told by holy men who talk of enlightenment and such nonsense that the past has got to come to a stop before you are free to operate in the "present" and so realize your potential or future possibilities. This I deny. First of all, why should you be interested in attempting to stop the past from interfering with the present? Be very clear that this idea that the past must die, that time must have an end, has been put into you by those self-appointed guardians of your so-called soul—the priests, holy men, and saviors of mankind. It is not yours at all. You need to be very clear also about the implications of ending the influence of the past. It is really a dangerous, calamitous thing. In your search to find the end of time, the past, you must use the past. So you only succeed in perpetuating the past. This is a fact, like it or not. Anything you do—having kinder thoughts, behaving selflessly, approaching life negatively rather than positively, listening to holy men, listening to me—is only adding momentum to the past. All the techniques and methods of achievement at your disposal are from the past, and, therefore, useless. Luckily, there is absolutely nothing to be achieved.

Yes, but I think most of us realize that real happiness is a by-product of something else, and cannot be achieved in and of itself.

Your actual approach to happiness is grounded in self-interest and naiveté. You are a pleasure seeker at all times, and therefore your ideal of the greatest happiness is simply one of endless pleasure without any pain. When you perceive, if you do at all, the absurdity of such an approach, you then say, "If I could find God and enlightenment I would be free from the contradictory desire to have the one (pleasure) without the other (pain)." So this then becomes your goal, which will take more time to achieve. You are back where you started.

To demand the cessation of the continuity of the movement of the past is ridiculous and unfounded. We have been brainwashed by all these people that if we free ourselves from the past in this life, everything will be hunky-dory, full of lightness and sweetness. It is all romantic hogwash, sheer unadulterated fantasy, and nothing more. You have fallen for this stuff, unfortunately. After all, what is it that you can do? All your actions are from the past. And anything you do only strengthens the hold of pleasure and pain upon you. Ultimately it is all pain and no pleasure. I can say that with certainty, but you are still cock-sure that there is a timeless state, a way out. It is therefore impossible for us to communicate. What I am saying will, if really listened to, put an end to you as you know and experience yourself. You are not listening to me at all. Your so-called listening is all in the past. The constant interpretation by the past of what is being said prevents you from listening to what is being said.

All I can guarantee you is that as long as you are searching for happiness, you will remain unhappy. This is a fact. Society is so organized and complex that you have no other way of surviving except to accept the way of life around you as organized, along with the limitations it places upon all of us. We must all accept the reality of society, whether we like it or not. But this is not what we are talking about. What we are talking about is altogether different. All your relationships, knowledge, and experiences, all your emotions and feelings, all that romantic stuff, belongs entirely to society, not to you. You are not an individual at all; you are secondhand people.

Only when you are free from what every man and woman has thought and felt before you will you become an individual.

Such an individual will not go around attempting to destroy everything that belongs to society. He is not in conflict with society at all. He would never tear down the temples and institutions or burn books that men have made with great care. He would not be a rebel. All the accumulated knowledge, experience, and suffering of mankind is inside of you. You must build a huge bonfire within you. Then you will become an individual. There is no other way. Society is built on a foundation of conflict, and *you are society.* Therefore you *must* always be in conflict with society. The real individual, one who is free of the accumulated tradition and knowledge of mankind, is necessarily a threat to that society. Society, of which you are a part, cannot be other than it is. So stop trying to save it or change it. You cannot even change your mother-in-law.

Not all of us are so obsessed with our own personal happiness and salvation. Many of us are socially, politically aware, and merely wish to create a new world, a differently organized society, so that poverty, injustice, and other social wrongs are corrected. You talk as if we all were fixated on only our own personal problems and goals, while in fact most of us want to be of service to the world and seek not selfish ends, but simply a better, more humane society.

You want to change yourself into something and at the same time find you cannot change at all. This "change" you talk of is really just more romantic fancy stuff for you. You never change, only think about changing. As long as you want to change, for some reason or the other, so long will you insist upon changing the whole world. You want a different world so that you can be happy in it. That is your only interest. You can talk of mankind, concern for mankind, compassion for mankind, but it is all bullshit, horseshit.

Since you are determined to bring about change—a notion put into you by your culture—you remain discontent and want the world to be different. When your inner demand to be something different from what in fact you are comes to an end, then the neurotic demand to change your society ceases. Then you cannot be in conflict with society. You are in perfect harmony with society, including its brutalities and miseries. All your attempts to change this brutal society only add momentum to it. This is not to say that the free individual is indifferent to society. On the contrary. In any case, it is you who are indifferent right now. You only talk and whine, meanwhile doing nothing. Sorry.

But it is very urgent that we have peace in the world.

Unless you are at peace with yourself, there cannot be peace around the world. When are you going to be at peace yourself? Next life? No chance. Wait, you will see. Even then there is no guarantee that your society will be peaceful. They will not be at peace. When you are at peace with yourself, that is the end of the story.

It seems that we have only this idea of a peaceful society, while actually our relationship to others is quite violent. How do we bridge this gap between the ideal and the actual?

You are trying to establish relationships with people around you, with society, with the whole world. For some reason or other the actual relationships are very ugly and horrible. Have you noticed that as long as our relationships satisfy the question, "What can I get out of this relationship?", as long as they can be directed to serve my personal happiness, there is no conflict? Every person is in the same situation—his relationships are harmonious as long as they serve his own ideas of happiness. And we also demand that our happiness be permanent. In the very nature of things this is impossible. There is no such thing as permanence at all. Everything is constantly changing. Everything is in flux. Because you cannot face the impermanence of all relationships, you invent sentiments, romance, and dramatic emotions to give them continuity. Therefore you are always in conflict.

So perhaps we should abandon the search for perfect, harmonious relationships and concentrate on understanding ourselves—is that it?

Understanding yourself is one of the greatest jokes, perpetrated on the gullible and credulous people everywhere, not only by the purveyors of ancient wisdom—the holy men—but also by the modern scientists. The psychologists love to talk about self-knowledge, self-actualization, living from moment to moment, and such rot. These absurd ideas are thrown at us as if they are something new.

This must be boring for you, responding to the same old questions wherever you go.

I have been everywhere in the world, meeting and talking with people. People are exactly the same the world over. The questions never vary. But I am never bored with it. How can I be bored? If I were some sort of fool getting some sort of kick out of this, looking for new, better and different questions, then there would be a possibility of getting bored. But I am not looking for anything, so boredom is impossible. Are you bored? You have no way of finding out for yourself.

I am bored because I am average, like everyone else. It is my mediocrity that makes life seem so empty and boring.

It is very difficult to be like the other fellow, to be ordinary. Mediocrity takes a great deal of energy. But to be ourselves is very easy. You don't have to do a thing. No effort is necessary. You don't have to exercise your will. You need not do a thing to be yourself. But to be something other than what you are, you have to do a lot of things. The boredom and restlessness you feel inside you is there only because you think you must be doing something more interesting, more meaningful, and more valuable than what you are already doing. You think that the way you are carrying on is terribly boring, and that there *must* be something more valuable, powerful, and exciting to do. So all this becomes part of the complex knowledge you have about yourself. The more you know about yourself the more impossible it becomes to be humble and sensitive. How can there be humility as long as you know something?

There is something in me that finds it difficult to be simple about all this. There seems to be a fear of...

All fears lead eventually to the fear of death, physical death. You are attempting to push the fear of death way into the background so you can continue, that is all. As long as you are fear-ridden, there can be no sense in discussing the meaning of life. Why ask questions and mystify life? You are alive because your parents had sex, period. Don't look for a meaning to life. There may not be any meaning at all. It may have its own meaning that you can never know. Obviously life has no meaning for you, otherwise you would not be here asking these questions. Everything you do seems absolutely meaningless, that is the fact. Don't bother about others. The whole world is an extension of you. The way you are thinking, feeling, and experiencing is exactly the same way everyone else in this world is thinking, feeling, and experiencing. The goal may be different, but the mechanism and instrument you are using to achieve your particular goal is not a whit different from that used by others to achieve theirs. Why should there be any meaning in living? The moment a baby arrives in the world it is interested in one thing—survival. The instinct in the baby to feed itself, to survive, and to reproduce itself seems to be the way of life. It is life expressing itself. That is all. You needn't impose a meaning upon it.

Living itself does not seem to be enough. We have aspirations and goals, and we feel that there must be a more sane and meaningful way of living.

Instead of living, you are obsessed with the question, "How am I to live?" That dilemma is put into us by our culture, and is the one responsible for many of our problems. Because you are dead, not living what we call life, you are concerned with *how* to live. If you succeed in getting rid of the idea of somehow living a better, nobler, and more meaningful life, you will replace that belief with another. You must face the fact that you know nothing about life or the living of it.

In spite of the fact that we are not living, we are terrified of death.

The body responds to life around it—the pulse of the heart, the various physiological processes, the throb of life all indicate the presence of life. When these processes stop, then what you call clinical death takes place. Next we observe the body breaking down into its constituent elements, in turn assuming new and different life forms. But this continuity of life in new forms is little consolation to you, for you want to continue in your present form, warts and all. If you bury the body, the worms have a field day. If you throw it into the water, the fish will have a feast. That life will continue no matter what. But you will not be there to experience death. There is only death in the clinical sense.

If I am not really living, if I cannot know death, if I really don't give a damn about society, if my life is actually meaningless, if my hard-won self-knowledge is just an expression of ignorance, then what I take to be reality is a projection of my own mind.

Where is this mind you talk of? Can you show it to me? There is no such thing as your mind and my mind. Mind is everywhere, sort of like the air we breathe. There is a thought sphere. It is not ours and not mine. It is always there. Your brain acts like an antenna, picking and choosing what signals it wants to use. That is all. You use the signals for purposes of communication.

First of all, we have to communicate with ourselves. We begin as children naming everything over and over again. Communicating with others is a little more complex and comes next. The problem, or the pathology if you will, arises when you constantly communicate with yourself, irrespective of any outside demand for thought. You are all the time communicating with yourself: "I am happy…I am not happy…What is the meaning of life?" and so on. If that incessant communication within yourself is not there, *you* are not there as you now know and experience yourself. When that inner monologue is no longer there, the need to communicate with others is absent. So you communicate with others only to maintain that communication you are having with yourself, your inner monologue. This kind of communication is possible only when you rely and draw upon the vast totality of thoughts passed on by man from generation to generation. Man has through the process of evolution learned to draw from this storehouse quicker, subtler, and more refined thoughts than the rest of the animals. They have powerful instincts. Through thinking man has enabled himself to survive more efficiently than the other species. This ability of thought to adapt is the curse of man.

Whether you lay it at the door of society, the genes, evolution, or the influence of the stars, it comes down to the same thing: we are all deeply conditioned and need to be free of that conditioning in order to function naturally and freely. This is obvious, isn't it?

It is not at all obvious to me. It is just not possible for you to be without conditioning. No matter what you do, you are conditioned. The "unconditioning" that the spiritual gurus are talking about is a bogus affair. The notion of being unconditioned, of unconditioning oneself, is just another item for sale in the marketplace of the holy business. It has no validity. You will find out. Anything you do is conditioned. Unconditioning yourself has no meaning. What you have to be free from is the very desire to be free from conditioning. Conditioning is intelligence, the ability to respond adequately to the environment. This is entirely unrelated to your fantasies, ideations, and mentations—what you take to be the heights of intelligence.

If inquiry, self-knowledge, and unconditioning don't help to solve my basic dilemma, then perhaps science can help through life-extension techniques or genetic engineering.

Even genetic engineering that the scientists are indulging in is not for the benefit of mankind. If they succeed, it will be handed over to the state. The state will use it to control everything and everyone. Brainwashing, which takes centuries, would be obsolete. Through a simple injection of genetically engineered substances into the body, the state can turn its citizens into bloodthirsty soldiers, mindless bureaucrats, or whatever type it wants.

Perhaps we are complicating it. Could it be that we are all just too shallow in thought, that we only lack sufficient vision and mental scope?

Forget it. In any event your actions must be destructive of man's ultimate interests, for they are born out of thought, which is a dead thing. Forcing life to fit your dead ideas and assumptions is your basic difficulty. Everything you stand for, believe in, experience, and aspire to is the result of thought. And thought is destructive because it is nothing more than a protective mechanism, programmed to protect its own interests at all costs. Anyhow, are there really thoughts? Are you thinking now? You have no way of knowing.

But it is a superhuman task to fully understand though, is it not? All religions and important philosophies have put before us a more or less superhuman figure who has somehow transcended the relative world—the world of thought if you will—and attained great heights. But we are ordinary men not capable of colossal, fearless, or intrepid actions.

If you are freed from the goal of the "perfect," "godly," or "truly religious" supermen, then that which is natural in man begins to express itself. Your religious and secular culture has placed before you the ideal man or woman, the perfect human being, and then tries to fit everybody into that mold. It is impossible. Nature is busy creating absolutely unique individuals, whereas culture has invented a single mold to which all must conform. It is grotesque.

So you are not a perfect man as some claim?

I wish I knew, but I don't want to bother. Who cares? I have no way of finding out, and if I did, it would be a tragedy for the world. They would make of me a model and attempt to live a certain way, creating a disaster for mankind. We have enough gurus, why add one more?

If you are not a teacher, a guru of some sort, then why do you talk to us? It appears to us that you are giving some kind of instruction, that you are expressing a teaching that can be of use to mankind.

I am just singing my song, then I go. If someone listens to me or not, it is not my concern. I don't consider any hypothetical situation. If nobody comes and talks, it is all right with me. Believe me, my talking is only incidental, it is not aimed at liberating anyone. I've been coming to this area for thirty years. If you are not here, maybe I'll watch the TV, or read crime fiction—it's all the same for me. I am not selling anything. This is so. I am simply pointing out that at the rate at which we are going the whole genetic engineering technology will end up in the hands of the political system to be used for the complete control and subjugation of man.

If this danger is really so imminent, then it is urgent that others "stumble" into their natural state, as you indicate happened to you, if for no other reason than to prove the existence of an alternative to genetic totalitarianism. Would you go along with this?

No. This natural state cannot be used to further anyone's crusade. Nor am I interested in setting myself up as an archetype or prophet for mankind. I am not interested in satisfying the curiosity of anybody. The scientists are making tremendous progress in the fields of microbiology and glandular and brain physiology. They will soon have enough sophistication in these areas to understand the physiological mutation that took place within me. I personally cannot make any definite statement except to say that the whole mechanism is an automatic thing. The interference of thought is not there anymore. Thought is functional in value, nothing more. It operates temporarily here when there is a demand from the environment, but cannot act with regard to becoming something or to changing things there. This is all. That is *energy*, an energy that can make functioning in this world sanely and intelligently an easy affair. Now you are wasting that energy by attempting to be something other than what you in fact are. Then you will have a certainty which cannot be transmitted by me or by anybody.

I have discovered for myself and by myself, that what we have been told about freedom, enlightenment, and God is false. No power in the world can touch this. This does not make me superior. Nothing of the sort. To feel superior or inferior you must separate yourself from the world. I do not look upon the world as a separate thing as you do. The knowledge I have about the world—whether within or without—comes into operation only when there is a demand for it. Otherwise I simply don't know. Your natural state is one of not knowing.

You make no special claims for yourself. Yet your listeners, including myself, sense a certainty and authority in what you say. Does not this indicate that you are in fact a free man?

The knowledge that you are this, that you are that, that you are happy, that you are unhappy, that you are a realized man, that you are not a realized man, is completely absent here. You, or I, have no way of knowing if we are free men. Nothing tells me that I am a free man. In your case the naming process, the wanting something, the questioning goes on and on no matter what.

Here thought functions only from a stimulus from the outside. Even then the response of knowledge is instantaneous, and I am back again like a big question mark. Your constant demand to experience the same thing over and over again results in compulsive, repetitive thinking. I don't see any need or reason for the repetitive process to go on and on. In my case there is no one separate from this functioning, no one who can step back and say, "This is reality." There is no such thing as reality at all. Reality is imposed upon us by culture, society, and education. Don't get me wrong, thought has a functional value. If we don't accept the world as it is imposed on us, we will end up in the loony bin. I have to accept it as a relative fact. Otherwise there is no way of experiencing the reality of anything. It is thought that has created the reality of your body, of your living, of your sleep, and of all your perceptions. You experience this reality through knowledge. Otherwise there is no way of your knowing for yourself that you have a body, that you are alive, that you are awake. All that is knowledge. The reality of anything is something which cannot be experienced by anybody.

We have found this talk most interesting. Thank you very much.

Thank you.

We Have Created This Jungle Society

I was reading your book the other day, U.G., and I must confess that I ended up with the feeling that all your arguments ultimately lead not towards hope, but the inevitability of human suffering and despair. Am I right?

Basically, I don't see any future for man. It is not that I am a doomsayer, but rather that anything that is born out of division in men will ultimately destroy him and his kind. So I don't dream or hope for a peaceful world.

Is that so because of the inevitability of violence?

Because the inevitability of war is in *you.* The military wars out there are the extension of what is going on all the time inside you. Why is there a war waging inside you? Because you search for peace. The instrument you are using in your attempt to be at peace with yourself is war.

There is already peace in man. You need not search. The living organism is functioning in an extraordinarily peaceful way. Man's search for truth is born out of this same search for peace.

He only ends up disturbing and violating the peace that is already there in the body. So what we are left with is the war within man, and the war without. It's an extension of the same thing.

Our search in this world for peace, being based upon warfare, will lead only to war, towards man's damnation.

Many philosophies, including Marxism, say that war and struggle are inevitable.

True, they are inevitable. The Marxists and others posit a thesis which, through struggle, becomes an antithesis, and so on. These are philosophical inventions devised to give life some coherence and direction. I, on the other hand, maintain that life may have started arbitrarily, it may have been put together by accident. Man's efforts to *give* life direction can only meet with frustration, for *life has no direction at all.*

But this does not imply that the missiles are on their way, that doomsday is just around the corner. Man's instinct for survival is very deep-rooted. What I am saying is that all this sweet talk of peace, compassion, and love has not touched man at all. It's rubbish.

What keeps people together is terror. The terror of mutual extinction has had a strong and ancient influence upon man. This is, of course, no guarantee. I don't know.

Now the problem is greatly increased by the fact that our technologies guarantee the extinction of all *life forms, not just man, in the event war breaks out at the higher levels.*

The day man felt this self-consciousness in him, which made him feel superior to every other species on the planet, is the day he set out on the road to complete and total self-destruction. If man is destroyed, probably nothing is lost. Unfortunately, the instruments of destruction he has been able to stockpile over the ages are getting worse and worse, more and more dangerous. *He will take everything with him when he goes.*

From where does this basic urge to assume mastery over himself and the world arise?

Its genesis was in the religious idea that man is at the center of the universe. For example, the Jews and Christians believe that everything is created for the benefit of man. That is why man is no longer a part of nature. He has polluted, destroyed, and killed off everything, all on account of his wanting to be at the center of the universe, of all creation.

But man has to belong somewhere, surely, even if it is not at the center of creation. The fall represents the beginning, not the end of man.

The doctrine of the fall comes in very handy for Christians, that's all; it doesn't mean a thing. The whole Christian tradition exploits this idea of Original Sin to the hilt, resulting in massacre, bloodshed, and such incredible violence.

Well, Eastern philosophies talk of a "still center" that can be found through meditation.

I question the very existence, the very idea of the self, the mind, or the psyche. If you accept the concept of the self (and it is a concept), you are free to pursue and gain self-knowledge. But we never question the idea of the self, do we?

What is this self you are talking of?

You are interested in the self, not I. Whatever it is, it is the most important thing for man as long as he is alive.

I exist, therefore, I am. Is that it? Descartes?

You have never questioned the basic thing assumed here. That is: "I think, therefore, I am." If you don't think it never occurs to you that you are alive or dead. Since we think all the time, the very birth of thought creates fear, and it is out of fear that all experience springs. Both "inner" and "outer" worlds proceed from a point of thought. Everything you experience is born out of thought. So, everything you experience, or *can* experience, is an illusion.

The self-absorption in thought creates a self-centeredness in man; that is all that is there. All relationships based upon that will inevitably create misery for man. These are bogus relationships. As far as you are concerned, there is no such thing as a relationship. And yet society demands not just relationships, but *permanent* relationships.

Would you consider yourself an Existentialist?

No, don't think you can put a label on me. The Existentialists talk of despair and absurdity. But they have never really come to grips with despair or absurdity. Despair is an abstraction for them.

But what about angst? Naufrage? Nausea? What was Raskalnikov feeling if not despair?

These are abstract concepts on which they have built a tremendous philosophical structure. That's all there is to it. What I refer to when I talk of self-centered activity is an autonomous, automatic, self-perpetuating mechanism, entirely different from what they are theorizing about.

You mean that the self survives mortality?

No. There is no question of a self there, so how can the question of immortality, the beyond, arise?

What beyond? Is there a beyond?

It is mortality that creates immortality. It is the known that creates the unknown. It is time that has created the timeless. It is thought that created the thoughtless

Why?

Because thought in its very nature is short-lived. So every time a thought is born, you are born. But you have added to that the constant demand to experience the same things over and over again, thus giving a false continuity to thought. To experience anything you need knowledge. Knowledge is the entire heritage of man's thoughts, feelings, and experiences, handed on from generation to generation.

Just as we all breathe from a common fund of air, we appropriate and use thoughts from the surrounding thought-sphere to function in this world. That's all there is to it. Man's insistence that thought must be continuous denies the nature of thought, which is short-lived. Thought has created for itself a separate destiny. It has been very successful in creating for itself a separate parallel existence. By positing the unknown, the Beyond, the immortal, it has created for itself a way to continue on. There is no timeless, only time. When thought creates time, a space is created there; so thought is also space as well. Thought also creates matter; no thought, no matter. Thought is a manifestation or expression of life, and to make of it a separate thing, impute to it a life of its own, and then allow it to create a future for its own unobstructed continuity, is man's tragedy.

But if thought can create matter, how do you explain phenomena like Sai Baba producing watches out of thin air?

It's just not possible. Sai Baba is a magician. He used to produce Swiss watches. But after the Indian government placed an import tax on Swiss watches, he soon began producing Indian-made watches. I saw a man on television the other day, who could make a jet aircraft disappear before your very eyes! Sai Baba conjures up a watch. He gives it to an honored disciple, but he, Sai Baba, receives all the acclaim and applause. It all looks legitimate, but is only a gimmick. I make fun of such things. How can you take them seriously?

O.K., then what do you take seriously? Life? Death? Extraterrestrial life?

I don't think that this kind of life exists anywhere else, on any other planet. I am not saying that there may not be life in other worlds; only that it is not like our existence here. Your ruminations about other forms of life and other worlds are just a wish for unlimited extension into the future and far-off places. Thought is trying to give itself continuity, and speculations about the future and undiscovered worlds are a convenient way to do it! Your thinking determines what you can become conscious of, period.

This all comes close to what J. Krishnamurti is saying. He says that the accumulated knowledge of man becomes tradition, assuming a continuity and legitimacy of its own. Don't you believe this?

No. I don't see how what I am saying is even close to his line of thinking. He talks of passive awareness, journeys of discovery, psychological transformations; opens schools and launches foundations. These activities do not free you, but perpetuate the movement of thought and tradition.

Is there any freedom of thought? Any freedom for man?

No, there is no freedom of action for man. I am not talking of some cataclysmic, deterministic philosophy of resignation, but...

There is no way out? Not even by contemplating one's navel? Not even by meditation? Not even by the raising of the kundalini? Not even by the conquest of illusion?

No. You can try all kinds of things, but it won't help. You will only succeed in creating disturbances within the body, disturbing the harmony that is already there. By bringing about strange hallucinations and unnatural metabolic changes you only harm the body. That's all there is to it. There is nothing you can do to reverse this, to change direction.

Not even a radical, even if temporary, break from tradition? If one could divorce one's actions from thought, one might be able to act without guilt, and without worrying about the consequences of one's actions. Action would be freed to do new, creative things perhaps.

What for? To be able to discover one's subterranean strengths? Thought-induced reality cannot be denied; it is *there*.

Some savants and seers have insisted that there are subtle energy centers within us that can be released by certain spiritual practices, including the concentration of the mind on precisely nothing.

In order to concentrate or focus on one thing you must block out the others. By concentrating upon what you take to be "nothing," you withdraw and separate yourself from the natural flow of life through and around you. You are part of a generalized magnetic field and what separates you from others is thought. You are concerned only with *your* happiness and unhappiness, the video set *you* are watching.

Isn't this unavoidable in light of the fact that each of us lives in a subjective world, no one seeing the "objective" world as it really is? When each of us looks at, say, that table there, each of us sees something different. So it is with all objects.

The table is not an object at all.
The very fact that you recognize the table as a table is the issue. It does not matter, as the philosophers seem to think, that you and I have slightly different views of the chair and so

interpret it differently. Neither does it matter whether the chair is there when I leave the room. The philosophers go on and on about this. It is absurd. You view and experience things from a different viewpoint than others, that's all. You think that you are having a subjective experience of an objective thing. There is nothing there, only your relative, experiential data, your "truth." There is no such thing as objective truth at all. There is nothing which exists "outside" or independent of our minds.

Even for the other fellow? Is his existence dependent only upon my mental activity? Is your wife or neighbor just an infra-psychic phenomenon?

Since I assume that "I" exist, he also exists. But I am questioning this. Do I have any way of experiencing the fact of my existence? I really have no way of finding out whether I am alive or dead. I could go to a doctor who will examine me, take my temperature, my pulse, my blood pressure, and he will tell me everything is normal. In this sense you're a living, animate being in contradistinction to the inanimate objects around you. But you have actually no way of experiencing *for yourself* and *by yourself* the fact that you are a living being.

Of course you can: you cut yourself, you bleed and experience pain; if you marry you suffer [laughs].

Yes, but there are two things. There is the body which feels the pain and the knowledge telling you, "This is blood," "This is pain," "This is the cessation of pain." There is pain, but there is no one there who feels the pain. There is nobody who is talking now.

I am not making a mystical statement when I say such a thing. Talking is a mechanical thing, like a tape recorder. Your questions draw out certain responses automatically. Whatever that is here comes out, that's all. Because you are asking questions, the answers are already there.

*What about love, deep abiding feelings, and profound responses to
the beauty of nature?*

Ha! All that typical romantic stuff. Pure poetry! Not that I have
any bone to pick with romanticism or poetry. Not at all. It just
doesn't mean anything. You actually have no way of looking
at the sunset because you are not separate from the sunset,
much less writing poetry about it. The experience you have, the
extraordinary experience you have when looking at a sunset you
want to share. Using poetry, music, or painting as a medium, you
attempt to share your experience with another person. That's
all there is to it. The actual sunset is beyond your experiencing
structure to capture. The observer is the observed. You cannot
separate yourself from what you see.

The moment you separate yourself from the sunset, the poet
in you comes out. Out of that separation poets and painters have
tried to express themselves, to share their experiences with others. All that is culture. Culture induces its own responses. There
is *nothing* more to it.

*What happens to an aboriginal who is untouched by civilization,
with no exposure to complex culture as you and I know it, and
responds to a beautiful sunset? How do you explain that?*

You see, it all depends on what we *mean* by culture. That part
of culture that promises you peace, bliss, heaven, moksha, and
selflessness is the problem. To separate the rest of culture—how
you entertain yourself, how you eat, your work habits, and language—from this counter-reality created by culture is a mistake.
The so-called savages are functioning in exactly the same way
we are functioning today. Basically, there is no difference. In
both the primitive and modern cultures there is no peace.

*So your message is that man cannot be at peace with himself. Is
that what you want to say?*

No. Man is *already* at peace with himself. The idea that there is peace somewhere else, sometime in the future, is causing the problem. All these religious experiences like compassion, bliss, and love are part of the craving for a nonexistent peace, which is destructive to the natural peace already there in the body.

No peace. No religion. No compassion. No hope. What does that leave us with U.G.?

Nothing. I am questioning the whole spiritual experience. That's what I am trying to rip apart.

What about the beautiful, ancient, and elaborate rituals that make up such a large part of our religious experience? Do they have any meaning or relevance to our lives?

Man has always wanted to entertain himself with something or the other. The rituals have provided him with the necessary entertainment over the years, and now they have been replaced by movies, videos, television, circuses, J. Krishnamurti talks, and the whole lot. There are many of them, you see. Each one is trying to sell his own particular brand of cigarettes, his own particular commodity. We want them. There is a market for these spiritual commodities. That is why someone is selling them. Nobody can sell me that kind of stuff because I'm not interested in it. Others may be.

Yes, but what are you interested in? What makes you want to carry on living?

Whatever is there. Whatever is happening at the moment is all that there is for me.

Come on. You're a here-and-now person, is that it?

No. To explain it that way is very misleading. I don't know how to explain it.

Look, I read science-fiction books. Why? Because there is action there. I am not interested in the outcome at all, only the ongoing action. It is like a striptease. It is the stripping I find interesting, not the ending. Who cares about endings? Similarly, all your yesterdays, all your knowledge, and your very sense of self are dead things of the past. These memories have a great deal of emotional content for you, but not for me. I am only interested in what is actually happening now, not tomorrow or yesterday.

Without the emotionally-charged memories of yesterday and the promise of tomorrow, there is little room for hope, is there?

To me there is no present either, much less the future. What is there is only the past, nothing else. So your phrase "the here-and-now" means nothing to me. At this moment there is only the past in operation.

I don't know if I make myself clear. If I recognize you and we carry on a conversation, it is only the past that is in operation. I am looking at things. If I recognize and name those things, the past is in operation. It is projecting what it knows. The future, although indeterminate, is a modified continuity of the past. So what is this "now" you are talking about? There is no such thing as this moment. This moment is not a thing that can be captured, experienced, or given expression to. The moment you capture what you think of "this moment," you have already made it part of the past.

All this implies that we can never touch the same place at the same time and place. It is like two tape recording machines in a room playing old tapes to each other. You have no way of communicating anything to anybody. There is no communication at all. And when this is understood very clearly there is no *need* for communication at all.

Which means that man's attempt to predict or preempt the future is condemned from the start, does it not? All this talk of communicating information, sharing knowledge, and interfacing is sheer bunk?

Yes, it is. For this reason man is denied any real freedom of action. You may prefer one kind of music or food over another, but that only reflects your own background and culture.

If what you are saying is true, then no one has any freedom of action, for everything one does has a cause, and all causes have a final cause.

Aha! Why do you assume that *everything* must have a beginning, an ultimate cause? Cause-and-effect may be just a casual thing. Events may just occur, just happen. The whole process of evolution may be just another happening, a causeless event. Why must you insist that everything *must* have a creator, that the whole thing must have sprung from some ultimate cause?

The most recent scientific evidence suggests that it all began with a Big Bang. Even explosions have a flash point. Things don't just go "bang."

That is *your* assumption. There may not be any such thing as the Big Bang. They use that term in contradistinction to the concept of creation in steady state. So these are two theories trying to establish themselves as truth. Each competes with the other, trying to present itself as the more plausible of the two.

But surely this is the way new ideas are born and tested within a rational community. It is a healthy thing, not a pathological thing, to seek truth and knowledge. It is a good thing in and of itself.

I am not against the scientific method per se. What I am pointing out is the fact that there is no such thing as a "pure" search for knowledge, or knowledge for its own sake. It is not so innocent. Knowledge is sought, scientifically or otherwise, because it gives power. Love is an invention of the moment, used to replace power. Since you have failed in every other way, through every other channel, to acquire that all-powerful state of being, you have invented what you call love.

So love is just another name for the power game? Is that what you want us to believe?

Exactly.

What about the kind of love Mother Teresa practices? What about compassion?

They are all born out of the divisive consciousness in man. Ultimately they will end up defeating the very cause they are working and dying for. The people around Mother Teresa are capitalizing on her fame. All they are interested in now is money, you know, to carry on her work. Why should all these things be institutionalized? You see someone in pain, hungry. You respond to him. That's all there is to it. So, why should that be institutionalized? You corrupt that feeling, the immediate response, which is not just a thought or petty emotion, when you attempt to institutionalize generosity and empathy. It is the immediate response to the situation that counts.

Institutionalization is the attempt to take a one-time situation and a one-time response and make out of them a continuous, predictable response. A single act of a good Samaritan becomes a way of looking at and doing things generally. Loving thy neighbor becomes a fact when everyone is doing it as a matter of course, not as a result of isolated acts of compassion.

I don't see that as compassion. That's the only thing you can do in a given situation, and that's the end of it. Animals are helpful to one another to a surprising degree. Human beings are naturally helpful to each other. When institutionalization dulls that natural sensitivity, I say it is not compassion. All events in my life are independent of all other events. There is nothing there lining them up or institutionalizing them.

Is this why you have steadfastly refused to allow your views to be propagated?

First of all, I have no views at all. You see, they wanted me to go on television in the United States. They have a program called Point of View. I told them "I have no point of view." I have no particular message for mankind, nor do I have any of the missionary zeal in me.

I am not a savior of mankind, or any such thing. People come here. Why they come is not my concern. They come out of their own free will and volition because they have heard of me or out of sheer curiosity. It doesn't matter. A person may come here out of any one of a number of reasons. He finds me somehow different, a rare bird, and cannot figure me out or fit me into any framework he knows. He tells his friends, and soon they arrive at the door. I can't tell them to get lost.

I invite them in, knowing very well that there is nothing I can do for them. What can I do for *you?* "Come in, sit down, make yourself comfortable," is all I can say. Some people make tape recordings of our conversations together. It is their concern, not mine. It is their property first of all, not mine.

I have no interest in asking the questions you are interested in. I have no questions of any kind, except those which help me to function in daily living: "What time is it?" "Where is the bus stop?" That is all. These are the simple questions that are necessary to function in an organized society. Otherwise, I never ask any questions.

Do you think this society is really organized?

This is a jungle we have created. You can't survive in this world. Even if you try to pluck a fruit from a tree, the tree belongs to someone or to society. So you have to become a part of society. That's why I always say that the world does *not* owe a living to me. If I wish to enjoy the benefits of organized society, I must contribute something to it. This society has created us all. Society is always interested in the status quo, in maintaining its own continuity.

Society has not created me. A simple act of lust created me.

That is true. But lust is born out of the thought of that individual who is part and parcel of society. The actual genetic information, probably residing in each cell of the body, is also passed on, and constitutes the basis of consciousness. What society is interested in is that we all contribute to the continuity of society, that we all perpetuate the status quo. Society will of course permit some slight modifications, but no more.

So, what does a man like me contribute to society? Nothing. So how can I expect anything from society? Society does not owe a living to me at all. On the other hand, what I am saying is a threat to society as it is presently organized. The way I am thinking, functioning, and operating is a threat to the present society. If I become a threat, this society will liquidate me. I am not interested in becoming a martyr or anything. That doesn't interest me at all. So, if they say, "Don't talk," fine, I don't *have* to talk.

So you don't have faith in man, like J. Krishnamurti does?

No, no. Not at all, not at all.

If they expect me to be a martyr so as to revitalize their faith in themselves, they will be sadly disappointed. It is their problem, not mine. If they find me a menace to society, what can they do? They may torture me, as they do in the communist countries. So what? Would I continue to speak against the state then? I really don't know what I would do. I do not indulge in hypothetical situations.

Would you have any political views? Do you have any political views about this society here? Do you believe in a specific form of government, taking sides on political issues?

I have views on every damned thing from disease to divinity because I have acquired all this knowledge through studies, travel, experience, and the like. But my views are of no more importance than those of the maid cleaning and cooking there. *Why* should any importance be given to my views and opinions?

You may say that I am a well-read man, and that, as a result of my reading, my travels, and my conversations with intellectuals, scientists, and philosophers, I have a right to express my views on everything. But nothing I say or believe is important. Do you understand that? All I am trying to point out is that all this knowledge you are so proud of flaunting isn't worth a tinker's damn.

Why has knowledge taken on such importance to us?

Because it gives you power. As I said at the very beginning, knowledge is power. *I know, you don't know. I have* religious experience and you *don't have* it. So it's all one-upmanship, showing off.

Does your past with the Theosophical Society contribute in any way to the sum total of your understanding of life? You know, all this astral business, Blavatsky's hocus-pocus, Leadbeater's buggery, the usual mumbo-jumbo of the Theosophical circus...

Whatever happened to me happened not because of, but *in spite of* that. And that's a miracle. I really don't know. I am not a man of humility or any such thing. Looking back on the situation, I really have no way of telling you what it was all about. All I know is that I am free from my past, and thank heaven for that.

Tell us, what do you think of "the sage who walks alone," J. Krishnamurti, the man you had the "falling out" with.

I think he is a tremendous hoax. That's what I have against J. Krishnamurti. He has never come out clean. If you ask him why not [come out clean], his argument would be that anything he says will become an authority for or against him. But that's a political position he has taken. In fact, he has already become an authority figure for hundreds and thousands of people.

And that's something you don't want to become?

No. I don't want to be that. Never. To me, the whole thing stinks.

But the chance to influence men, to change history...

No, never. That's what I am saying.

Is it that you reject using your power now that you have it, or is it that you reject the idea, the very principle of power over others?

It is the understanding, it is the knowledge which has dawned upon me. I cannot communicate it, much less recommend it to others.

Naturally. But if one wants to operate outside the whole corrupt field of power games, mustn't one be truly humble?

No. Humility is an art that one practices. There is no such thing as humility. As long as you *know,* there is no humility there. The known and humility cannot coexist.

In saying this I am not giving you a new definition of humility. I believe there is no such thing as humility at all. I'm just not in conflict with society. So, to create the opposite of the brutality in the world—humility—does not occur to me. Society cannot be anything other than what it is. So, since there is no demand to bring about a change *in* me, there is no corresponding demand to change society. I am not a reformer. I am not a revolutionary either. In fact, there is no such thing as revolution. All that is bogus. It is another commodity to be sold in the marketplace, to hoodwink gullible people.

In other words, there is no difference between the world of Gandhi and the world of Ho Chi Minh, or between the values Christ propagated and those Lenin fought for?

That's right. No difference at all.

Tell me something. J. Krishnamurti told me during a conversation that his entire worldview survives because he looks at life from a detached viewpoint. He is not the first one to say this. Many great men of religion and art have said the same thing. Do you agree that he sees most clearly who stands apart?

Did Krishnamurti say this, or did his followers say this?

He claims to have no followers.

First of all, I have no worldview, no structure of thought that can help you.

But you have perhaps created a structure of thought which helps you.

Nothing helps me. This certainty I have is something that cannot be transmitted to anyone else. And yet this certainty has no value at all.

How did you arrive at this certainty?

I stumbled upon it. You see, my grounding was in Madras, in the same kind of environment that produced J. Krishnamurti. I was surrounded by religious people, all kinds of strange people. I realized early on that they were all fakes whose lives and preachings were miles apart. So it [the environment] wasn't worth anything, as far as I was concerned. I know all about these saviors, saints, and sages. They have all cheated themselves and fooled everybody. But you may be sure that I am not going to be fooled by anybody. I am in a position to say they are *all* wrong.

The "change," if that is the word you want to use, that occurred to me is a purely physiological event, with no mystical or spiritual overtones at all. Anybody who gives a religious slant to any physical happening like this is kidding himself and is kidding the whole of mankind. The more clever and cunning you are, the more successful you will be in persuading people. So you acquire power from people, then project it upon others. You get tremendous power from your followers, then project it back on them. So it gives you the illusion that it is affecting everyone around you. You then come out with some ridiculous statement that this has affected the whole of human consciousness. Actually, it has no psychological or social content at all.

It is not that I am antisocial. As I have said, I am not in conflict with society at all. I am not going to destroy all the temples or churches, or burn any books. No such thing. Man cannot be anything other than what he is. Whatever he is, he will create a society that mirrors him.

Yes, but how did you stumble upon such wisdom?

Aha! That's the question!

You obviously don't get it by sitting under a tree in the moonlight.

No, there is nothing to get.

I refer not to some romantic achievement, but to that certainty you possess. You have a certainty, that's all. I feel that I and others don't have it. Neither do I know how to get it.

You must find your basic question. My basic question was: "Is there anything behind the abstractions the holy men are throwing at me? Is there really anything like enlightenment or self-realization?" I didn't want the question. I just had it. So naturally I had to experiment. I tried so many things, this, that, and the other for a while. Then you find out one day that there is *nothing* to find out at all! You reject them completely and totally. This rejection is not a movement of thought at all, not a superficial denial. It is not done to attain or achieve something.

Like the need to get something spiritual?

There is nothing to get. There is nothing to find or to find out. The understanding that there is nothing to understand is all there is. Even that is an inferential statement. In other words, there is nothing to understand.

The fact that there is nothing to understand is a certainty for you, but not me.

First of all, you see, you don't have the hunger, the thirst to find out the answer to that. So you can't do a thing about it. Anything you do perpetuates that, keeps your hunger at bay. What seems to have happened to me is not that my hunger has been satisfied either with bread crumbs or a whole loaf of bread, but that the hunger found no satisfactory answer and burned itself out. All these thirst-quenchers haven't helped to quench my thirst. But somehow in my case the thirst burned itself out. I am a burnt-out case—but not in the sense in which you use that term. It's an entirely different kind of being burnt-out.

What is there now is something living. There is no *need* for communication; no communication is possible on that level. The demand to know, to be certain, is not there at all.

I don't understand.

It's just like the tree out there. What do you want to do with the trees? They are not even self-conscious that they are useful to other forms of life, providing shade. Like the tree, I am never conscious that I can be of service to anyone.

Don't you have any simple honorable sentiments like affection for another, love, or even lust? Haven't you ever seen a beautiful woman and wanted to make love to her?

The movement of desire is so fast that it doesn't stop there. There is something—I wouldn't say it's more interesting or more attractive—but it changes that movement and demands your complete attention. Everything happening at that moment demands your complete and total attention. In that state there are no longer two things—lover and beloved, pursuer and pursued. What you call "a beautiful woman"—which is an idea—gives way to something else. And there comes a time when you can't love her in the old way any more.

You mean when you see a beautiful woman you are totally involved without having to get involved?

The thought that she's a woman isn't there. Then you see what a beautiful woman can give you. "What can I get from this woman?" is not there. Everything is constantly moving. There is no religious content to this at all.

Forget about religion. We are talking about beautiful women. They affect you in a different way, you say. You don't exhibit the obsession with sex which so many of us do when in the company of beautiful women. Yet you are affected. I am obsessed with beautiful women and sex, and want to reduce the impact they have on me. How can I get some objectivity on the matter, as you seem to have?

It's too much of a hassle to bother about that. Please remember that...

Don't you think that an individual who has seen the light should lighten the way for others? Don't you feel some sense of responsibility for your fellow beings? Isn't it incumbent upon you to share with the world the truth you have "stumbled upon"?

No. I have no way of transmitting it and you have no way of knowing it.

Yes, but don't you want to inspire the world around you?

Inspiration is a meaningless thing. So many things and people inspire us, but the actions born out of inspiration are meaningless. Lost, desperate people create a market for inspiration. So, I am not interested in inspiring anybody. All inspired action will eventually destroy you and your kind. That's a fact!

Is there any way of preventing that? Is not life the only cure-all?

What do you want to prevent? In you love and hate are born. I don't like to put it that way because love and hate are not opposite ends of the same spectrum; they *are* one and the same thing. They are much closer than kissing cousins.

If you don't get what you expect out of the so-called love, what is there is hate. You may not like me to use the word "hate," but it is apathy and indifference to others. I believe love and hate are the same thing. I tell this to people wherever I go, all over the world.

Every year you spend four months in America, four months in India, and four months in Switzerland. That is dangerously close to the usual travel plans of J. Krishnamurti, isn't it? He covers an almost identical route year after year.

I don't know why *he* is doing that. It is the weather that is responsible for my movements. When it is hot in India, I go to Switzerland. When it gets too cold in Switzerland, I move to California, then back to India again. This whole J. Krishnamurti thing no longer interests me.

Perhaps. But you must have observed the entire thing very carefully because you were a part of it for a long while. Everyone knows of your past interest in J. Krishnamurti, and the fact that you eventually broke with him.

In the early days he didn't have a huge organization like he has today. It was a small simple organization publishing a few books, that was all. He did a little traveling and public talking, organized informally by some friends. That was it. But now it is a limited concern, a growth industry like any other business. This kind of organization he has now, with worldwide real estate holdings, boards of trustees, vaults of insured tape recordings, millions of dollars, all runs counter to his basic teaching, which is that you can't organize truth. He shouldn't be building an empire in the name of spirituality.

Have you ever met any of the "God-men" of India? You know, the famous ones making a fast buck in the holy business.

No, I've never been a shopper. I've encountered a few of them for a few minutes in my travels, that's all.

What I am was born out of my own struggle. I learned everything about myself by myself. Both the secular and the spiritual schools of thought irritate me. The gurus and God-men are, therefore, of no interest to me at all. We have exported them to the United States and Europe. They have their own too.

Yes. The Reverend Moon, Jim Jones, scoundrels galore...

And now there is another Jones: Da Jones, "the one who gives" in Sanskrit. Any holy scam is welcome there, whether from Indonesia, Japan, India, or from Nepal. If they get popular enough in the West, make enough of a splash, we bring them back to India. It is similar to how Indian women bring back saris from the West to wear here. They pay three times the price there!

Have you ever met Maharshi Yogi in Switzerland?

No, never. I don't go out of my room, so I can't say. I'm not in touch with what's going on here in India. I don't care for the newspapers here, so I don't read them. Indian current events don't interest me, you see, because whatever happens here has no real effect on the world. India is not in a position to affect the world. Although, there is no sure way to divide up opinions into spiritual, political, or otherwise. You may call this a political opinion.

How can India give direction to or influence the world? India has neither the power nor the moral status. The spirituality you claim does not actually work in the life of the country. You have to show the world that the oneness of life you have preached for centuries operates in the daily life of this country, as well as in the lives of individuals. That is difficult.

No one is interested in what India says or does. It doesn't have the necessary stature to affect world events. The only thing about India that interests the rest of the world is the question, "What will happen to her millions and millions of people? In which direction, towards what camp, is she going to move?" Nothing else.

Does a religion like Marxism help? It has a spiritual content, after its own fashion. It seems to look at a broader, less archaic frame of reference.

Marxism as a religion has failed. Even Maoism is dead. Even the Marxist countries are looking for a new God now. They have lost faith in man and are once again looking for a new God, new Church, new Bible, and a new priest. The search is on for a different kind of freedom.

But Hinduism allows a great deal of freedom. It was never a conservative religion, like Christianity, Islam, or Marxism.

The only difference between the East and the West is the difference in our religions. Christianity has not produced such weird characters as we have in this country. Here religion is an individual affair. Each one has set up his own shop and is selling his particular wares. That's why we have the variety here, which is lacking in the West. This variety is the most attractive part of our so-called heritage.

Hinduism is not a religion. It is a combination and confusion of many things. The actual word "Hindu" comes from a lost non-Sanskrit word no longer in use. You wouldn't know anything about it. The invading Aryans who set up the Brahmanic social structure found the native Indians to have a dark complexion and called their religion the religion of the blacks—the "Hindus." The scholars and pundits may not like my interpretation, but it is correct and historical.

Again, I repeat, Hinduism is not a religion in the usual sense; it is like a street with hundreds of shops.

You mean Rajneesh's sex shop next to J. Krishnamurti's awareness shop, which is next to Maharshi's meditation shop, which is next door to Sai Baba's magic shop, which is next to...

Basically they are all the same, exactly the same. Each claims that his wares are the best to be found in the market. Some products, like Pears Soap, have been in the market so long that people have come to know, depend upon them, and consider them superior to others. The durability of a particular product doesn't mean very much.

What is your opinion of the Indian entertainment business? They say most of your following comes from this industry.

Everything in this country is entertainment. The politicians thrive on the gullibility of men. Religions thrive on the credulity of others. Well, we are damn fools, you see. That's all there is to it.

With such an opinion of mankind, you must not have any high hopes for the future of the race.

I don't think anything better will happen *to man, or for man.*

But surely the incredible progress of technology, especially in the West, in the last hundred years, bodes well for man.

That is true. But that is because of the industrial revolution. Nations like Russia, America, and other Western nations have taken advantage of the industrial revolution to push technology ahead.

Man seems to have made more progress in the last one hundred years than he did in the previous four billion years.

That's exactly what I am saying. It is because of the industrial revolution that far-reaching changes are sweeping the world. How effective these changes will be is anybody's guess. The regime of science and technology is already slipping.

Where do you think all this will take us?

Why should it take us anywhere? Why? What for? "Progress" means "to advance into enemy territory." You are hopeful that unbridled progress will bring a solution to our problems. If it was that clear-cut, we might as well program the computers and see what they have to say regarding our future and our destinies.

But if we are nothing more than the sum total of our past, the prediction becomes easy and accurate.

This will give us no guarantee as to where the future will lead.

No, we have control over our futures.

Something unexpected and unpredictable happens and the whole course is suddenly changed. We take it for granted that we can channel life in the direction we want, but there is no guarantee we will succeed. Events are really independent of one another. We create and put them together. We have created the philosophical structure of thought, but that does not mean that there is a pattern or purpose for everything. Nor does it mean that everything is predetermined.

But what about hope? Surely man lives by hope.

Man has always lived in hope and will probably die in hope. In the light of the tremendous destructive power he now has at his command, he will probably take every other form of life with him when he goes. This is not my doomsday song, but when you look realistically at our situation this seems to be the lot of us all, like it or not. You are mistaken if you think or hope that we can put the whole momentum of human history on a different track. We need to be saved from those saviors who promise the millennium just around the corner.

How can you help it?

The "how" creates another savior.

Yes, but is there any other way of changing course than the spiritual?

First of all, you see, to divide life into the material and the spiritual has absolutely no meaning to me. All this hogwash about spiritual life is born out of the assumption that there is a spirit which has an independent existence of its own. The assumption makes no sense.

What about the notion that the body is destroyed, but the spirit lives on?

It's just a belief. It doesn't mean anything at all. I have no way of transmitting this certainty to you. There is nothing that will rise or reincarnate itself after I die. For you to speculate on the beyond has no meaning.

The body itself seems to seek a kind of immortality through procreation.

That is the nature of life. The demand for survival and the need to reproduce oneself is inherent in the nature of life. Your sexuality, your progeny, your family structure, and so much more is an extension of this basic natural drive to survive and procreate.

So when you die you are finished?

If, when this body is buried, the memories people have of me are buried along with it, that will be the end of me.

Some of your followers want to scatter your ashes.

What for? Very often people ask me, "Are you not going to leave any instructions on how we should dispose of your dead body?" What the hell! Who wants to leave any instruction? It will begin to smell and become a nuisance to society. It's not my problem, but society's. I am already in hell. There is no need for me to die to reach there.

You have a family somewhere, don't you?

My daughters, two of them, are in Hyderabad. One of my sons, Vasant, died recently of cancer. The other fellow, Kumar, is younger and was born in America. He is an electronics engineer there now. I see him occasionally when I visit the U.S.A. I don't have much contact with my family. They come and visit me sometimes. That's all. I have no emotional links with them, or with anybody for that matter. Not even with Valentine, the old Swiss lady I have been with for the last twenty years. I don't think I have any emotional links with anybody.

Have you ever had any emotional links with anybody?

I don't know. I probably did not, even with my wife with whom I lived for twenty years. I really don't know what kind of links one should have.

You've never had any overwhelming feelings towards another person, man or woman?

What obsessed me most was to find out the answer to my question. It was the one overriding thing for me. What was *behind* the abstractions these people, including J. Krishnamurti, were throwing at me? If there is nothing there, how could they have created all this mischief in the world? I understood that you could kid yourself and others, but I wanted an answer. I never got an answer. The question just burnt itself out.

That does not mean that I am enlightened, or that I know the Truth. Those who have claimed such things have fooled themselves and others. All of them are wrong. Not that I am superior to them or any such thing; it is just that they are making claims that have no real basis at all. That was and is my certainty. There is no power in the world that can make me accept anything. So I am not in conflict with the power structure. I am not interested in taking anything away from anybody.

We sense a kind of remoteness or disinterestedness in you. Haven't you ever been carried away by anything, say, a beautiful woman, a beautiful sunset, or a beautiful piece of music? Has nothing ever totally swamped you and made you want to go away from everything, I don't know where to...

Whatever else I may or may not have been, I've never been a romantic in that sense. All that is romanticism for me. Romanticism is not my reality. Nothing has ever, or will ever, sweep me off my feet. It is not that I am the opposite of that, a man of reason. It is the element of reason in me that revolted against itself. I am not anti-rational or arational, just unrational. You may infer a rational meaning in what I say or do, but it is *your* doing, not mine. I am not interested in anyone's search for happiness, romance, or escape.

It could be more than mere romanticism. It could be a self-abandonment, a crazy, frenzied, or a terrifying, magnificent, spiritual, or sexual experience.

There is no experience here. So, how can there be these dramatic, crazy experiences? I have no way of separating myself from events; the event and I are one and the same. I'm sure you don't want me to say any crude things as far as sex is concerned. It's just a release of tension. I don't romanticize at all about this kind of stuff. As I once told my wife, "Don't talk of love and intimacy to me; what keeps us together is sex. The problem is that I, for some reason, cannot have sex with another woman. That is my problem. I have no way of freeing myself from this problem." I don't know if all this makes any sense to you. All this talk of love never meant anything to me. That's the end of this obsession with sex.

But at one stage you did make love with another woman.

Yes, but that was a situation not of my own making. I won't say I was seduced. It doesn't matter whether one seduces another or is himself seduced. The fact is you did it. It was not *that* person who was responsible. I myself was responsible. It was a peculiar kind of auto-eroticism that was involved in this case.

How can you say that?

I was *using* that person. It is a terrible thing to use somebody to get pleasure. Whether you use an idea, a concept, a drug, or a person, or anything else, you cannot have pleasure without *using* something. This revolted me. What are you laughing about? This is my life, take it or leave it.

I am not interested in using, influencing, or changing any-body. This is a statement on what I am, how I lived, nothing more. This will not be of any tremendous value for mankind and should not be preserved for posterity. I don't believe in posterity. *I have no teaching.* There is *nothing* to preserve. Teaching implies something that can be used to bring about change. Sorry, there is no teaching here, just disjointed, disconnected sentences. What is there is only your interpretation of either the written or spoken word, nothing else. The answers you get are yours. They are your property, not mine. For this reason there is not now, nor will there ever be, any kind of copyright for whatever I am saying. I have no claims.

Tell me, U.G., what was your childhood like?

My mother died when I was seven days old. My maternal grand-parents took care of me. My grandfather was a Theosophist. He was a wealthy man and instilled a strong religious atmosphere around the house. So, in that sense, J. Krishnamurti was also part of my background. They had his picture on every wall; I could not avoid him. I did not go to him in search of anything. He was just part of my background. It would have been remark-able had I never gone to see him. My problem was to free myself from the whole background that was strangling me. That's all.

Where did you grow up?

Mostly in Madras, in the Theosophical Society. I went to the University of Madras. I lived most of my formative years with and amongst the Theosophists.

Did they repel you from the very beginning?

From the very beginning, in a way. But I continued to fend for myself. I wanted so much to free myself from my past. I tried *so* hard. After J. Krishnamurti walked out on the whole thing I eventually broke from them [the Theosophists] also.

Do you have memories of Annie Besant?

Oh, yes! She was a remarkable woman. I met her when I was fourteen. I remember her oratory. My grandfather was very close to Annie Besant. She was an institution. I think India has every reason to be thankful to her, in more respects than one. But the modern generation doesn't know a thing about her. Neither do they know much of Gandhi. It is difficult to say how much people now remember about him. This new film on him will probably spark some interest in his life.

What do you think of Gandhi's beliefs?

You want my opinion. I will freely give it. For some reason or other I never liked him. Perhaps it was my Theosophical background. Above all, he was a mixture of a saint and a politician. I think he was the only man amongst the whole lot who really tried to model his life after what he professed to believe in. He may have failed—he *has* failed in my opinion—but the fact that he tried to live according to the model he had before him, made him an interesting chap. Many others besides him were instrumental in gaining India's freedom. What he has left this country is nothing. It is a sentimental thing to give lectures on him every year on his birthday. He and his followers talked everlastingly, but, as the new film shows, he used violence from start to finish.

But you can also say that of Christ, Buddha, and Mohammed. It is those who come after a great teacher that misapply his teachings.

You cannot exonerate the founders and leaders of religions. The teachings of all those teachers and saviors of mankind have resulted in only violence. Everybody talked of peace and love, while their followers practiced violence.

There is something funny about the whole business. It was this gap between word and deed that signaled to me early on that something was very wrong. I felt that the teachings were wrong, but I lacked certainty. I had no way of brushing them aside, putting them entirely out of my consciousness. I was not ready to accept any of them on sentimental grounds. Even when my efforts to be rid of them resulted in episodes of Christ and Buddha consciousness, still I was discontent. I knew that there *must* be something wrong somewhere. This was really my problem, you know.

You reject things on both sentimental and rational grounds. What is left?

It is like the man who is riding a tiger and is thrown off. The tiger, maintaining its own momentum, continues on—it's gone. That's all there is to it. You cannot do anything with the tiger anymore. So you never again have the fear of encountering or riding the tiger. It is finished. It has gone.

So I think there is little point in my doing anything in society—it has its own momentum. Anything you try to do will engulf you and add to that momentum. Who has given the mandate to all these people to save mankind? Compassion and love are two of their gimmicks.

Did you ever meet that strange old Theosophist called Leadbeater during your Theosophical days?

Yes, I met him. He was also part of my background. He never impressed me very much. I am aware that there were rumors that he was a homosexual. It doesn't matter to me. Sex is a part of life. Homosexuality, lesbianism, heterosexuality, it's all the same. I don't have *any* moral position. Society, which has created all these sociopaths, has invented morality to protect itself from them. Count me out. Society has created the "saints" and "sinners." I don't accept them as such.

There can be error, mistakes, weakness, but no sin for me. I personally see no reason why we should bother with the Bible, the Koran, the Gita, or the Dhammapada[11]. We have a political body with its civil and criminal codes. That should be sufficient to handle the problem.

The Body *as a* Crucible

You are operating under a great many assumptions. The first assumption is that you think all human beings are exactly the same. I maintain that no two individuals are the same. Your attempt to arrive at the greatest common denominator is self-defeating.

As scientists we want to find out if there is a uniqueness behind the apparent similarities in people. We are interested in human dissimilarities and exceptions. The yogins and religious leaders seem to offer us cases of really exceptional and unique persons. We want to study them, and you.

Don't you have any other way of finding out than going to these yogins and claimants who are peddling their wares in the marketplace? The second-raters may submit to your scrutiny, but the real McCoy, if there is one, will never submit to your tests. This will be a very big problem for you. You can't get a J. Krishnamurti, a Sai

Baba, or a Muktananda to cooperate. Those you can get to act as guinea pigs are cheaper by the dozen.

But then how are we to go about finding the basis of inner transformation?

I don't know. I would suggest, however, that you give no credence to the claims these people make. Everything must be tested.

That is the whole point: we are trying to find a way to test their credibility on a scientific basis.

I am afraid that you are making a horrendous mistake by even toying with the idea of giving *any* consideration to the claims that these people make. Everything must be tested.

The only thing we have to work with is the statistics and data of what we call "normalcy," nothing more.

The answers to this problem, as all your problems, have to come from *you,* not from these yogins and meditators. You may be making a tremendous mistake. This is what I tell the Western psychologists also. You have no objective relationship with the data and knowledge you collect. Your constant interpretation of data means that you are involved in what you are studying; there is no separate entity. It is the interpreter that is of the greatest importance.

But, of course, it's possible and necessary to study man.

He has to understand himself first. Are the data and knowledge—and the theories you derive from them—going to help in this regard? From the point of view of knowledge, there is no way of understanding yourself. The computer machine never asks itself, "How am I functioning?" Really understanding yourself demands not the mere accumulation of data, but a quantum jump. I like to use the example of Newtonian physics. Within the Newtonian framework, things work in a certain way. Another scientist eventually comes along who is able to drop the Newtonian assumptions and thereby is able to perceive a whole new dimension of physics. Just as Newtonian principles eventually became a strait-jacket strangling creative thought, so your data about human uniqueness bars your looking at things, including yourself, anew.

I like to use the example of Picasso. He had the same problem—he wanted to break new ground, find new techniques. He achieved a breakthrough and eventually became a model for others. Very cheap artists are now imitating his style. So, one day, Einsteinian physics will have to step aside for a fresh system of knowledge. I submit that nature is attempting to create a unique individual every time something is created. Nature does not seem to use anything as a model. When once it has perfected a unique individual, that individual is thrown off the evolutionary process and is of no further interest to nature.

This is why whatever I am, whatever I say, cannot be duplicated by another. Therefore, being incapable of transmission, it has no social value. Nature has no use for me, and neither has society. By using the models of Jesus, Buddha, or Krishna we have destroyed the possibility of nature throwing up unique individuals. Those who recommend that you forget your own natural uniqueness and be like someone else, no matter how saintly that person may be, is putting you on the wrong track. It is like the blind leading the blind.

When dealing with these yogins and holy men the first wrong turn you take is in trying to relate the way they are functioning with the way you are functioning. What they are describing may not be related to the way you are functioning at all. Uniqueness is not something which can be turned out in a factory. Society is interested only in the status quo and has provided all these so-called special individuals so that you'll have models to follow. You want to be like that fellow—the saint, the savior, or the revolutionary—but it is an impossibility. Your society, which is only interested in turning out copies of acceptable models, is threatened by real individuality because it [individuality] threatens its continuity. A truly unique person, having no cultural reference point, would never know that he is unique.

But isn't it possible that the very presence of a unique person, a fully flowered individual, can be of some help to others, not in the sense of providing a model, but in possibly triggering change and uniqueness in others?

I say no. Because the unique individual cannot reproduce himself either physically or spiritually, nature discards him as useless. Nature is only interested in reproducing, and from time to time throwing out a "sport" or unique specimen. This specimen, not able to reproduce itself, is finished with evolution, and is not interested in making of itself a model for others. That is all I am saying.

Don't you feel that that throwing up of uniqueness by nature is the flowering of uniqueness for the individual?

That is bound to happen in individuals who, through some chance or accident, manage to free themselves from the burden of the entire past. If the entire collective knowledge and experience of man is thrown out, what is left is a primordial and primeval state without the primitiveness. That kind of individual is of no use to society at all. Like a shady tree, this individual may provide shade, but can never be conscious of his doing so. If you sit under the tree, a coconut may fall on your head; there is a danger involved. For this reason society may feel threatened by this individual. This society, structured the way it is, can make no use of such a person.

I don't believe in lokasamgraha, the helping of mankind, compassion for the suffering world, lifting a little of the heavy karma of the world, and all that kind of thing. No one appointed me savior to mankind.

So, you are saying, are you not, that no scientific approach, yogic approach, or meditative approach, can have any relationship to the uniqueness and freedom you are talking of, is that it?

I will tell you a story about that. When I was young I did Yoga in the Himalayas for seven years with Sivananda Saraswati. It didn't help, so I dropped it. After my "calamity" in 1967 I felt that my body could not endure the tremendous outbursts of energy taking place there. So I conferred with a friend, Sri Desikachar, who was a yoga teacher. He said, "I don't know if I can be of any help. Perhaps my father (Dr. Krishnamacharya of Madras) may be able to help you." So I practiced some yoga techniques for a second time. But I soon found for myself that the whole yoga business runs counter to the natural way the body is functioning. I tried to discuss it with them, but what I said did not fit into Patanjali's Yoga Sutras[12], so we could not communicate. Eventually, I announced to them that I was dropping my yoga practice. When once the organism has freed itself from the stranglehold of thought, anything you do to try to bring about peace and harmony there only creates disharmony and violence. It is like using war to create peace in a peaceful world. When the search itself comes to an end, it comes to an end with a big bang, as it were. Then peace is something that cannot be practiced or taught.

I don't think that we are really interested in any such big bang. We want some wisdom, some serenity.

So, a hungry man is satisfied with some crumbs thrown at him. Soon he wants a full loaf and is promised such by the holy purveyors in the marketplace. It is not a question of satisfying hunger. Hunger must burn itself out without knowing satisfaction. The hunger, and the search it entails, is the problem.

If you drop the fictitious models of the saint and holy man, you are left with the natural biological arrangement. The separative structure of thought, which was introduced into the consciousness of man long ago, has created the violent world, and will probably push man and the rest of life on this planet to the brink of extinction. But biologically each cell has the wisdom to avoid models and promises, and simply, out of sheer survival motives, cooperates with the cell next to it. Out of the terror of annihilation, man, like the cells of his body, will learn to cooperate, but not out of love or compassion.

Behind this biological cooperation and the flowering of individuality is there not some transcendental thing trying to come out?

I don't think so. It is highly individualistic, not in the usual sense as defined by culture, but in a different way. The control of the body through thought has destroyed the possibility of humans growing into complete humans, that's all. You may dispense with the notion, so prevalent now, that awareness can help bring about any qualitative change in you. Nature is trying to create a unique individual there. The potential is already there in you. But somewhere along the line mankind got off on the wrong track and there seems to be no way out.

In relation to the flowering of individuality, the question that keeps arising is, "Why not me?"

Just forget it, you haven't got a chance. There is nothing you can do. I don't know what to advise you to do. You are stuck. Perhaps the geneticists and microbiologists will come up with the answers. I can assure you that the holy business won't help you one bit. Further, if the state gets a hold of the means to do genetic engineering, they will use it to take away the last vestiges of man's freedom. Then that will *really* be the end of it.

It is possible to use, again, the simile of the computer. They, the computers, have become so sophisticated now that they are thinking and self-correcting themselves. We may, someday, just have to plug them in and then follow their advice. If you could let your body function like a computer you would have it. The extraordinary intelligence of the biological organism is all that is necessary for good living, but we are all the time interfering with its natural operation through the medium of thought. Your "natural" bodily computer is already programmed, pressed, and plugged in! You don't have to do a thing! We are a very long way from this primal condition. Somehow, you see, something hits you like lightning and burns the whole thing there. This man then is neither sinner nor saint; he is far outside the framework of society.

So, all we can practice, if that is the word, is non-interference?

Trying to stay out of the way implies that you are waiting for something marvelous to happen. Such waiting prevents the possibility of anything happening. I am telling you all this from my own experience. For forty-nine years I searched for a man called "U.G." The whole culture put me on the wrong track. I tried the dead gurus as well as the living gurus. Eventually, I realized that the search was useless, that the "enemy was me." Now the entire knowledge, and the search it engendered, has been thrown out of my system completely.

And you feel no obligation to help others to understand this thing?

It isn't a marketable commodity, sir! It is simply the absence of a false demand which has been put in there by society and culture. The demand to change one's self and the demand to change the world go out of the system together. I am neither antisocial nor thankful to society. I don't feel any bounden duty to play any part or to help my fellow men. All this kind of thing is balderdash.

So wanting to change the world, no matter how noble one may feel about it, is a self-centered, egotistic activity. Is that what you are saying?

The man who is trying to free himself from the world, or from what he calls "evil" is actually the most egotistical of men. The shattering perception that finally dawns on you is that there is no such thing as "ego" at all! This insight blows everything apart with a tremendous force when it hits you. It is not an experience that can be shared with another. It is not an experience at all. It is a calamity in which both experience and the experiencer come to an end. A man in such a state does not escape reality and has no romantic tendencies. He harbors no humanistic notions about saving the world, for he knows that anything that is done to save it only adds momentum to it. He knows that there is *nothing you can do.*

But we must go on living and acting. How can we conceive of action that does not add momentum to the chaos of society?

That's just another concept. Your actions and the consequences of those actions form one single event. It is the logical, cause-and-effect thinking that imposes a sequence to events. The sudden evidence of light and the throwing of the light switch which "preceded" it are actually one thing, not two. They appear to you as two or more events only because time has created a space between. But time and space, apart from the ideas of "time" and "space," do not exist at all.

Creation and destruction are going on simultaneously. The birth and death of thought happen simultaneously. That is why I insist that there is no such thing as death at all. Even the body does not die; it can change form but does not cease altogether. Because death really does not exist, it is impossible for you to experience it. What you do experience is the void or emptiness you feel upon the disappearance of someone's body. Death can never be experienced, and neither can birth for that matter. In your natural state, where the body is allowed to function without the interference of thought, birth and death are going on all the time.

In this natural state you are talking of, are there any psychological entities, any personalities, egos, self, or identity at all?

There are no persons, and no space within to create a self. What is left, after the continuity of thought is blown away, is one disjointed and independent series of interactions. What happens in the environment around me, happens in here. There is no division. When the armor you are wearing around you is stripped away, you find an extraordinary sensitivity of the senses that responds to the phases of the moon, the passage of the seasons, and the movements of the other planets. There is simply no isolated, separate existence of its own here, only the throb of life, like a jellyfish.

Can you describe a little of this recurring death process you go through?

It, of course, defies description. But I can mention that in this death state, the ordinary breath stops entirely, and the body is able to "breathe" through other physiological means. Among the many doctors I have discussed this strange phenomena with, only Dr. Leboyer, an expert in childbirth, gave me a sort of explanation. He says that newborn babies have a similar way of breathing. This is probably what the original word *pranayama* meant. This body goes through the death process on a daily basis, so often that, in fact, every time it renews itself it is given a longer lease. When, one day, it cannot renew itself, it is finished and carted off to the ash heap.

This death process is yoga, not the hundreds of postures and breathing exercises. When the thought process stops splitting itself in two, the body goes through a clinical death. First the death must take place; then yoga begins. Yoga is actually the body's skill in bringing itself back from the state of clinical death. This is supposed to have happened to a few people, like Sri Ramakrishna and Sri Ramana Maharshi. I wasn't there and have no interest or resources to find out if this is so. This yoga of renewal is an extraordinary thing. If you observe a newborn baby, you will have observed the way it moves and articulates its whole body, all in a natural rhythm. After the breath and heartbeat come to almost a complete stop, somehow the body begins to "come back." The corpse-like appearance of the body—the stiffness, coldness, and ash covering—begin to disappear. The body warms up and begins to move, and the metabolism, including the pulse, picks up. If you, out of scientific curiosity, wish to test me, I am not interested. I am simply making a statement, not selling a product.

So, it is much more like the Chinese Tai-Chi than classical Yoga *asanas*. The movements and postures that the body performs when breaking down the stiffness left over from the death process are beautiful, graceful movements, like those of a newborn baby. Yogins now prescribe *savasana,* the corpse posture, *after* the performance of any moving postures. This is backward. You start yoga as a dead stiff body; then the body is renewed through natural rhythmic movements. Probably there was some guru who went through this natural death process and his disciples, watching him return to life, tried to duplicate this death process though breathing and posture techniques. They got it backward. First, you must die, then, there is yoga.

This whole process of dying and being renewed, although it happens to me many times a day, and always without my volition, remains very intriguing to me. It just happens out of nowhere. Even the thought of the self or ego has been annihilated. Still there is *something* there experiencing this death. Otherwise, I would not be able to describe it here.

With the absence of any demand to repeat or use this death process, the senses are given a field day. The breath, no longer under the domination of the separative thought structure, can respond fully to the physical environment. Upon seeing a beautiful mountain or sunset, the breath is suddenly drawn out of you, then back in, all in a natural rhythm. This is where the expression "breathtaking beauty" probably comes from. The only way you become conscious of things happening around you is through subtle changes in breathing patterns. It is a tremendous mechanism, and in it there are no persons, no things.

So this non-lung breathing is epiphenomenal to the death process, a side show as it were?

Not necessarily. Sometimes you are just sitting there and you suddenly feel a shortness of breath, almost a gasping for air. It is something like a second wind. The yogins are trying to achieve this second wind through the practice of various techniques. So do the athletic runners. If you watch the runners you will see that they have to pass a "wall" of exhaustion and shortness of breath. Once through the "wall" they are running on a second wind. It is something like that for me. But even this passes, and finally breathing stops altogether and the body bypasses the lungs, breathing with the pulse of the body alone. Sometimes, when there is nobody to talk to, I sit and allow all these strange things to happen.

Haven't western doctors attempted to describe the glandular changes that accompany this death process?

Yes, but there is little understanding of this kind of thing in the annals of Western medicine. One paper, done by Dr. Paul Lynn of the United States, stresses the difference in the way my thymus gland functions. But there are other glands that are affected also—the pineal, the pituitary, and others. The pineal gland, which controls the whole movement, breathing, and coordination of the body, is greatly affected. When the separative thought structure dies, these glands and nerve plexuses take over the functioning of the organism. It is a painful process, for the hold of thought over the glands and plexuses is strong and has to be "burnt" off. This can be experienced by an individual. The burning or "ionization" needs energy and space to take place. For this reason the limits of the body are reached, with energy lashing out in all directions. The body's containment of that energy in its limited form brings pain, even though there is no experiencer of pain there.

This painful death process is something nobody—not even the most ardent religious practitioners and yogins—wants. It is a very painful thing. It is not the result of will, but is the result of a fortuitous concourse of atoms.

How all this fits into your scientific structure, I do not know. Scientists doing work in this field are interested in these changes, if they are described in physiological rather than mystical terms. These scientists envisage this kind of man as representing the end product of biological evolution, not the science-fiction superman or superspiritual beings. Nature is only interested in creating an organism that can respond fully and intelligently to stimuli and reproduce itself. That's all. This body is capable of extraordinary perceptions and sensations. It is a marvel. I don't know who created it.

Scientists in the field of evolution now think that the present breed of humans we have on this planet probably evolved out of a degenerated species. The mutation that carried on the self-consciousness must have taken place in a degenerate species. That is why we have messed everything up. It is anybody's guess as to whether anyone can change the whole thing.

Is it possible that a survivor of this total death process, a mutant of some sort, could change the course of human destiny, so to speak?

The claims they make have really no basis at all, for they speak of affecting the whole of human consciousness. I think that human consciousness in its totality is a tremendously powerful thing, with a strong momentum of its own. I don't think they realize what they are talking about. The whole of human consciousness is a very formidable thing. The only consciousness they know of is that created by thought. The thinking consciousness of man can only be affected by propaganda, persuasion, or drugs. Any change from these sources is only within the old framework, and, therefore, useless. What can we change? Is change necessary? What for? I don't know.

It sounds as if a certain soil is needed to grow the kind of mutants you describe. We are all brought up in barren, mediocre, and unnourishing soil. Will not some other soil help?

The sensitivity is still there, despite the poor soil. The whole blueprint is there, like in the plant sitting over there. If you don't water and nourish it, it dies. Nothing is lost for mankind. Don't attempt to develop new soil compositions. That is what we have done with the trees and plants, and we are now polluting the whole planet. The same would happen with trying to cultivate a better strain of mankind.

From the way you describe it, there must be a radical change in the source of one's identity after the collapse of the separative structure. Is there a self that remains after the "explosion"? Is the "I" only in the brain?

There is no "I." "I" is only a first person singular pronoun. The totality of the thoughts, feelings, experiences, and hopes of mankind constitute the "I." It is a product of the past. That "I" is a symbol of the totality of man's consciousness. Actually, there is no separate, discreet psychological entity there, only the word "I." Similarly, there is only the word "mind," but no such thing as *your* mind and *my* mind. So the word "mind" has created us all for the simple reason that it needs each of us to maintain its continuity. The separative structure of what we call "the mind" vitiated the natural survival mechanism of the body to the extent that our society has pushed it to the limits of tolerance. The H-Bomb is an extension of the policeman there hired to protect me and my property. It is no longer possible to draw a line between the two. But the survival of the separative structure guarantees the eventual destruction of the physical organism.

Why is it that your words do not trigger some radical action in us?

What opportunity that might have been there is already lost because whatever has been said here has already been appropriated by and become part of your old framework. Your so-called sensitivity to what has been said does not go very deep.

Everything that was standing as an obstacle before is still there. In fact, it has been strengthened by this conversation. The self will use *anything* to perpetuate itself; nothing is sacred. If you *do* try to go deep and demolish what is there, it is *only* with the idea and purpose of constructing a new superstructure.

Why do you assume that?

Because that's the way it works.

Suppose I am serious about it and somehow find out...

No suppositions, please! What happened to me was acausal; it just happened. In spite of all my efforts, struggles, and intentions, this thing happened to me, and that is the *miracle of miracles.* You cannot make this happen. It is not subject to duplication because when it hits you, it hits you at a time and place never before touched by life. It is not an experience at all, and, therefore, cannot be communicated or transmitted. It is not something you share. It is a rare bird, that's all. All you can do is to put it in a museum and look at it, but you can never duplicate or share it.

It is frightening to think of living without a center, a self, a reference point.

The reference point, the "I," cannot be eliminated through any volition on your part. In the final analysis, it is your genetically predetermined program, your "script." To be free of that miserable genetic destiny, to throw away the "script," demands tremendous courage. You have to brush *everything* aside to find out. Your problem is not how to get something from somebody, but how to reject everything that is offered by anybody. There is, in fact, no "how" to it. This demands a valor that comes before courage, for its existence implies the occurrence of something great—the impossible. No amount of cultivation, of either meekness or courage, will be of any help whatsoever. There is not a thing you can do, for this thing is of one's entire being, and anything you do is fragmentary, partial. You must be helpless.

When I sit here and my eyes are open, the whole of my being is the eyes. It is a tremendous "vista-vision," with everything passing through you. Your looking is so intense and undistracted that the eyes never blink and there is no room left for an "I" that is looking. Everything looks at me, not vice versa. As it is with the eyes, so it is with the other senses, each having an independent career of its own. The sensual response, which is all that is there, is not modified, censored, or coordinated, but left alone to vibrate in the body. There is a sort of coordination that arises when the organism must function for survival and smooth mechanical operation. Only enough coordination is allowed which is essential to respond to a given situation. Then things lapse back into their independent, disjointed rhythm.

Do not translate what I am saying here as "bliss," "beatitude," or "enlightenment." It is actually a frightening, bewildering situation. It has nothing to do with so-called mystical or transcendental experiences. I see absolutely no reason why a religious or spiritual slant should be given to it at all. I am describing nothing more than a simple physiological functioning of the human organism. Although all this is not apart from nature, it will never fit into any nature study or scientific form of knowledge.

So you have to reject everything?

Not reject. The thing you are rejecting, and the rejection itself, have no relevance to the actual way your organism is now functioning. When that is seen clearly, there remains nothing to reject or renounce. You are prepared to reject so that you can get, that's all. Your Upanishads say that it must be the object of your fondest and highest desires. But I emphasize, on the contrary, that the desire itself must come to an end. It is the search itself, no matter how noble you may think it to be, that is disturbing you. Forget about the petty little desires you have been advised to control. When the desire of desires is dispensed with, the others are of no importance.

You are not saying that because what happened to you cannot be scientifically appreciated in all its fullness, that ordinary events, things, and people cannot be appreciated fully, are you?

Certainly not. Within that framework everything is valid, relatively valid. But the "reality" you want to study is put together by the psyche or self, and I emphatically deny both. Therefore your search for reality, psychological authenticity, and self-realization is meaningless to me. They are the products of frightened people. The scientific procedure, not the self, gives you a reference point so that you may measure the truth or falseness of what I am saying.

Look, I tried everything to find an answer to my burning obsession: "Is there such a thing as enlightenment at all, or have we all been fooled by abstractions?" That utter frustration and complete failure to answer that question created an intensity. The first third of my life was spent in India around Theosophists, J. Krishnamurti, yogins, holy men, sages, Ramana Maharshi, the Ramakrishna Order—in short, all the associations that could benefit a person interested in spiritual matters. I found out for myself that it was all bogus; there was nothing to it at all. Totally disillusioned with the whole religious tradition of both the East and the West, I plunged myself into modern psychology, science, and whatever the material world could give me. I found out for myself that the whole idea of spirit or psyche was false. When I experimented with and studied the material world, I was surprised to find that there was no such thing as matter at all. Denying the spiritual and material basis of things, I was left with nowhere to turn. I began drifting on my own, unable to find an answer from any source. Then one day the futility of what I was doing dawned upon me, and the question which had obsessed me for almost my entire life got burnt, then disappeared. After that there were no more questions. The thirst burned itself out without ever satisfying itself.

Not answers, but the ending of questions, is the important thing. Even though everything got burnt there, still embers remain to express themselves in a natural rhythm. What impacts this expression may have on the society around me is not my concern.

Glossary

Ahimsa
> Non-violence.

Asana
> Lit. seat. A physical posture. One of the eight "limbs" of Patanjali's yoga.

Ashrama
> A spiritual retreat.

Atma
> Lit. the Self. The interior self as distinguished from the empirical self which one experiences in everyday life. In the Upanishads and Advaita Vedanta, Atma is believed to be non-different from Brahman, the ultimate reality of the universe.

Avatara
> Lit. incarnation (usually of God). Sanskrit term for a Savior or a saint.

Bhagavan
> Lit. God. Also a form of addressing a liberated person, as such persons are believed to attained divinity.

Chakras
> The nerve plexuses or centers along the spine and in the

head through which the Kundalini (see below) energy is led.

Guru

A teacher, particularly of the spiritual kind.

Japa

Lit. muttering or whispering. A muttered prayer consisting of reciting (and repeating) passages from scriptures, spells or names of a deity.

Jivanmukti

Liberation during one's lifetime.

Karma

The effects of a person's past actions on his or her present and future state.

Kundalini

A form of yoga practiced in India, primarily in the school of Tantra. The term means "serpent power," the energy which is believed to lie dormant in the human being and which through breath control and other means is made to travel through various chakras (see above) along the spine to be ultimately united with universal energy or Godhead in the Sahasrara Chakra (the thousand-petaled lotus) located in the top of the head.

Lokasamgraha

Lit. welfare of the world. Also the act of saving the world.

Mahatma

Lit. a great soul. The title of a spiritually enlightened person.

Mantra

A series of syllables, considered sacred (and sometimes magical), used in meditation and rituals.

Moksha

Sanskrit term for liberation.

Nirvana

Lit. blowing out. Buddhist term for the extinction of the ego leading to enlightenment.

Pranayama
> Breath control. One of the eight "limbs" of Patanjali's yoga. Consists of controlled inhalation, retention, and exhalation of air.

Puja
> Devotional ritual and prayer.

Pundit
> A learned man. Also used as an honorary title.

Ram nam
> A mantra ("the name of Rama"), the repetition of which is used as part of meditation.

Sadhana
> Spiritual practice.

Samadhi
> Deep meditative trance state.

Samskara
> Psychological conditioning or impressions from past lives.

Sanskrit
> The classical language of India in which most religious and spiritual literature was composed.

Savasana
> The corpse posture. One of the asanas (see above), consisting of lying on the back and relaxing all limbs.

Swami
> Lit. master or lord. A form of addressing spiritual teachers or one's favorite deity.

Vedanta
> A system of Hindu monistic or pantheistic philosophy based on the Vedas.

Yoga
> Lit. joining or union. In general, a path to liberation. More specifically, the system of physical and mental discipline and meditation propounded by Patanjali, the practice of which is believed to lead to liberation.

Endnotes
by Terry Newland

1. The family name is Uppaluri, while the given name is Krishna-murti, given to him after his grandfather's name, and which means, in Sanskrit, "the very image of Krishna." It is a common name for boys in south India and indicates no family relationship between him and the famous teacher and author, J. Krishnamurti.

2. Valentine was a remarkable woman in her own right. Born in Switzerland in August, 1901, the daughter of a famous Swiss brain surgeon (after whom the deKerven's Syndrome is named), she crossed the Sahara Desert on a motorcycle, was the first woman to wear pants in Paris, was the first woman movie producer in France, and tried (unsuccessfully) to join the fight against Franco's fascists in Spain.

3. There seems to be some kind of connection between U.G. and the famous philosopher Jiddu Krishnamurti. Born in May, 1895, not far from U.G.'s place of birth, in the State of

Andhra Pradesh, south India, J. Krishnamurti was "discovered" by Annie Besant, the well-known President of the Theosophical Society. She and others in the Society became convinced that the little Brahmin boy was the new world teacher, or gadget-guru. Setting him up at the head of a worldwide organization dedicated to propagation of his teaching, he was soon traveling the world talking on his general theme of individual freedom through awareness, unbiased inquiry, and intense scrutiny of what is. He apparently underwent some sort of profound psycho-physical transformation in his early thirties in Ojai, California. He soon thereafter broke, at least formally, with the Theosophical Society and the Order of the Star, the principal organizations that embraced and promoted his messiahhood, and began a new life as a private citizen. For many years he lived quietly, counseling individuals, giving a few informal talks, and participating in educational work. In the late '50's his books "The First and Last Freedom" and "Commentaries of Living" created a minor sensation and a much larger and more generalized following. He rejected any leadership role, as well as attempts to institutionalize his teaching, to his unqualified good credit. In the late '60's he and others launched the huge Krishnamurti Foundation, headquartered in Brockwood Park, England.

The similarities between U.G. Krishnamurti and J. Krishnamurti are, according to the former, illusory. "Other than our names," says U.G., "I don't think we have anything in common." They were both born into Brahmin, Theosophical, south Indian families; they both were long associated with the Theosophical community, especially at Adyar Madras, the religion's world headquarters; they both use similar language in denouncing the prevailing theological and psychological assumptions of both the east and the west; they live in the same places in the world at approximately the same time; they both, whether they approve or not, have a devoted following, each indubitably convinced that their man is unique among teachers.

I do not know J. Krishnamurti's thoughts, if he has any, on U.G. But the latter's view of the former may be of interest to those wishing to contrast these two powerful and unique figures. In his youth, U.G. was surrounded by admirers of J. Krishnamurti, and himself developed a profound, though not unmixed, respect for the man. U.G. was later to say, "I thought that he might be the only one who had really freed himself from his background and had found what I was looking for. For a time I and my wife visited him in Madras. We had long serious talks, but got nowhere. I was left with the feeling that he had seen the sugar cube, but had never tasted the sugar cube." Whatever J. Krishnamurti's state, it was clear that he could be of no help to U.G. After his calamity U.G. took a hard line against the older man, calling him "the greatest fraud of the 20th Century," and "a purveyor of archaic, outmoded, outdated, Victorian hogwash." He has never questioned the man's personal integrity, but feels that he has contradicted the very fundamentals of his own teaching. "He denounces systems and opens meditation schools, talks of the crippling effects of conditioning then runs schools which foster more conditioning, talks of simplicity and builds worldwide real estate organizations; says you must be on your own, then takes measures to preserve his teachings for the future," says U.G. Further, U.G. insists that J. Krishnamurti has subtly enticed people into believing in a spiritual goal, a goal which moreover can be reached through specific techniques—"passive awareness," "free inquiry," "direct perception," "skepticism," etc. J. Krishnamurti talks of transformations in consciousness, while U.G. rejects the idea of transformation altogether. "There is nothing to be transformed, no psyche to revolutionize, and no awareness you can use to improve or change yourself," says U.G.

4. Referring to Jiddu Krishnamurti.

5. Referring to J.K.

6. Mandukya Upanishad: One of the principal Upanishads, officially forming part of the larger scriptures of the Hindus called the Vedas.

7. Samkara: The Vedanta philosopher of the 8th century Kerala, India, who propounded the non-dualist philosophy based on the Upanishads. This philosophy teaches that Brahman (Ultimate Reality) alone is real, that the world is an illusion, and that there is no difference between Atman (the interior self) and Brahman.

8. Bhagavad Gita: One of the major scriptures of Hinduism. Officially part of the epic Mahabharata. Teaches different paths to union with God (or liberation) including "disinterested action."

9. Gowdapada: (c.780 A.D.) The philosopher who revived the monistic teaching of the Upanishads. His pupil Govinda is the teacher of Samkara, the famous Advaita (non-dualist) philosopher. He is the author of Mandukya-karika, a commentary on the Mandukya Upanishad.

10. Brahmasutra: A central scripture of the Vedanta religion.

11. Dhammapada: A Buddhist classic, officially a part of the Suttapitaka, one of the three "baskets" containing the teachings of the Buddha collected about the third century B.C.

12. Patanjali's Yoga Sutras: The aphorisms of Patanjali's yoga. The work contains discussion of the yoga conception of liberation and the means to attain it.

About the Author

U. G. Krishnamurti was born in India in 1918 to Brahmin parents and was given a rigorous education in classical Hindu literature. He was raised to become a great spiritual teacher, in a manner similar to J. Krishnamurti (to whom U. G. is not related), as his family believed that he had approached enlightenment in a past life. As a young man, U.G. attended the University of Madras and studied widely in psychology, science, and philosophy. He became a popular lecturer for the Theosophical Society, an organization that introduced Eastern spiritual wisdom to the West, founded in 1875 by Madame Blavatsky. At age 25, U. G. married and eventually fathered four children.

U. G. continued lecturing throughout the world. Then in 1961 he began to feel that he was no longer in control of his life. He left his family and went to London without means or purpose. As he describes it, "I was a bum practically, living on the charity of some people and not knowing anything. There was no will. I didn't know what I was doing. I was practically insane." This seemingly aimless period of his life lasted for six years, marked by an intense interest in the question, "What is that state?" He was still trying desperately to understand the state described by all the great spiritual teachers, by Shankara, Buddha, and Jesus. Eventually he came to believe that he was in that state, and that became the basis for his radical philosophy.

U.G. Krishnamurti died in March, 2007.

Sentient Publications, LLC publishes books on cultural creativity, experimental education, transformative spirituality, holistic health, new science, ecology, and other topics, approached from an integral viewpoint. Our authors are intensely interested in exploring the nature of life from fresh perspectives, addressing life's great questions, and fostering the full expression of the human potential. Sentient Publications' books arise from the spirit of inquiry and the richness of the inherent dialogue between writer and reader.

Our Culture Tools series is designed to give social catalyzers and cultural entrepreneurs the essential information, technology, and inspiration to forge a sustainable, creative, and compassionate world.

We are very interested in hearing from our readers. To direct suggestions or comments to us, or to be added to our mailing list, please contact:

SENTIENT PUBLICATIONS, LLC
1113 Spruce Street
Boulder, CO 80302
303-443-2188
contact@sentientpublications.com
www.sentientpublications.com